GREAT BRITISH SPIRIT

GREAT BRITISH SPIRIT

Acts of
of kindness
and heroism

JOHN BLAKE

First published in the UK by John Blake Publishing
An imprint of Bonnier Books UK
80–81 Wimpole Street, London, W1G 9RE
Owned by Bonnier Books
Sveavägen 56, Stockholm, Sweden

www.facebook.com/johnblakebooks
twitter.com/jblakebooks

First published in hardback in 2020

ISBN: 978-1-78946-387-3
Audio Digital Download ISBN: 978-1-78946-398-9

British Library Cataloguing-in-Publication Data:

A catalogue record for this book is available from the British Library.

Design by www.envydesign.co.uk

Printed and bound in Great Britain by Clays Ltd, Elcograf S.p.A.

1 3 5 7 9 10 8 6 4 2

© Text copyright Charlotte Browne

John Blake Publishing is an imprint of Bonnier Books UK
www.bonnierbooks.co.uk

INTRODUCTION

What comes to your mind when you hear the phrase British spirit? From fortitude to self-deprecation and even curtain twitching, the term continues to conjure up a mix of deeply ingrained responses, impressions and memories. The British are renowned the world over for keeping their upper lip in check. But, when it comes to sharing their thoughts regarding what they believe defines British Spirit, they're not immune to displaying pride and, maybe, even a little emotion.

For music lovers, it's the cheeky humour of The Beatles in their early days – ready with quick-fire quips for a reporter who's asked yet another irreverent question about the length of their hair. For sport fanatics, it's Olympic legend Kelly Holmes winning two gold medals at Athens 2004, after a decade of setbacks and disappointments. For comedy fans, it's *Dad's Army*, which set the template for a host of pompous and incompetent characters in the British comedy canon. British spirit means many different things to many different people.

But the theme of courage in adversity, in all its many and

varied forms, is a frequent mention – whether that's sitting defiant in deckchairs on British coastland, as thunder rumbles overhead; or a little isle refusing to submit to the biggest bully in Europe, who has the rest of the continent by the scruff of its neck.

When success is achieved against all odds, all the better. Would Kelly Holmes's victory at the Olympics have meant as much if she hadn't overcome all the obstacles to get there? The swell of support on central court for Tim Henman and Andy Murray over the years proves how much love the British hold in their hearts for the underdog. Indeed, Britain itself was once the underdog, of course, at a time when the country's spirit was pushed to its limits.

Historians today – and even British people at the time of the outbreak of World War II in September 1939 – challenge the idea that Britain stood entirely alone. Within days Canada, Australia, New Zealand and South Africa had issued declarations against Nazi Germany, and in the subsequent years, hundreds of thousands of servicemen from Britain's Empire joined the Allies to fight.

But eight months into Britain's phony war, France and Belgium fell to the Nazis in May 1940. As Churchill ordered the mass evacuation of British and French troops from Dunkirk, the situation for Britain looked undeniably bleak. The country was under enormous pressure to yield and make a pact with Nazi Germany. Churchill always stated publicly that negotiations were out of the question. However, there is evidence he secretly feared the country would lose the Battle of Britain and that there would be no other alternative but to concede.

As Churchill made his rallying call to arms to parliament on

28 May 1940, he knew that the stakes were incredibly high. He couldn't have been more prescient when he declared that 'disaster and grief' would be the price to pay for 'the ultimate defeat of our enemies' – nothing could ever eclipse the six years of pain, suffering and loss that followed and World War II would become the deadliest global conflict in recorded history. But Britain's refusal to give in, during the war's early days, meant the eventual victory felt all the greater on that sunny day in May 1945.

In more recent years the term 'blitz spirit' has been criticised as a propaganda tool that undermined the psychological trauma many families suffered during the bombings, in favour of servicing the government narrative that the British resolve could not be broken. No doubt, there is some truth in this. But as many people who lived through those extraordinary times will attest (without any guarantee of a future existing beyond that evening) they still had a choice in how to react to their current set of circumstances, no matter how horrific they were. Perhaps the British spirit could be defined as displaying this attitude – whether that's singing 'roll out the barrel' in the underground during an air raid or knitting clothes out of dog hair for evacuated children. As many of the people in this book prove, we have some choice in how we react to any challenging circumstances we find ourselves in. We can make a difference, however large or small, through personal or collective action.

However, there are problematic issues surrounding the British spirit that we continue to grapple with. Ever since the Huguenots fled to Britain from France in the 17th century, the country has enjoyed a reputation as a safe haven for people fleeing persecution and tyranny. In turn, over the centuries, Britain has benefitted greatly from the variety of skills, trade and culture each new wave of immigration has brought. But it's not surprising that the extent of Britain's tolerance was brought into question, especially in the years that followed World War II.

In 1948, Caribbean migrants from the West Indies began to arrive to help rebuild post-war Britain. The majority were former service personnel who'd fought in World War II and were granted citizenship under the British Nationality Act of 1948. But for many of these migrants – who continued to arrive throughout the 1950s and 60s – the welcome they received in Britain's largest cities was about as warm as the accommodation they were afforded by local authorities. Signs stating: 'No Irish, no Blacks, no Dogs' decried Britain's reputation for humanity, tolerance and fairness.

Activist and campaigner Paul Stephenson was born in Britain and served in the RAF in the 1950s. In 1963, he led the Bristol boycott, which helped pave the way for the first piece of legislation in Britain to prohibit racial discrimination. He is just one of the campaigners featured who fought, and continue to fight, for change in our society. In the process, they also continue to push the parameters of what it means to be British, while championing a British spirit that no one is excluded from and that we're all proud to be a part of.

Many of the people featured in this book chose to do extraordinary things in extraordinary circumstances, and for no personal gain. No one forced Edith Cavell to risk her life smuggling British and Belgian troops out of enemy territory in Belgium during World War I. No one coerced Nicholas Winton into wrestling with bureaucracy at the Home Office to secure the safe passage of over 600 Jewish children from Nazi-occupied Czechoslovakia to the UK. They could have simply looked the other way and chosen to do nothing. And no one would have ever reproached them for it. But they, along with many other people in this book, chose to act, often for no greater reason than they believed it was the right thing to do.

Some of them helped people affected by injustice or inequality in society; whether it was happening hundreds of miles away from them or on their own door step – from the founder of Save the Children Eglantyne Jebb, who was committed to alleviating the suffering of all children (regardless of their nationality), to Max Levitas who campaigned for decent air-raid shelter provisions in the East End during World War II.

Some faced ridicule or the destruction of their career for daring to go against the grain – as in the case of Manchester's medical officer Dr Niven, whose radical proposal to shut down schools and public buildings, to reduce the spread of Spanish Flu, defied medical advice of the day. Many opposed him. But Niven's refusal to back down or discard his beliefs saved the lives of hundreds of thousands of Mancunians.

Others refused to let ignorance or fear halt progress or keep certain taboo subjects shrouded in secrecy or shame. Duncan Guthrie was determined to find a way to fund research that would help find a cure for polio, while Chad Vrah provided a lifeline for people who felt they had nowhere else to turn, when he founded The Samaritans.

There are people here who showed exceptional courage and bravery. Some of them paid for it with their lives – Special Operations Executive agents Violette Szabo and Noor Inayat Khan, POW Tom Kirby-Green, and flight attendant Barbara Harrison, who helped passengers evacuate a burning aircraft at Heathrow Airport.

Other stories prove how life-changing a simple kind act or gesture can be – there are those who refused to walk on by when they witnessed a person on the verge of ending their life. Their kind words instilled hope and not only prevented the death of a person but set them on a different path in life.

In more recent times, we have seen an outpouring of kindness in our communities. The Covid-19 pandemic and subsequent lockdown at the beginning of 2020 compelled us to retreat and take shelter, yet also look beyond our immediate needs and reach out to people in our neighbourhoods.

Many have drawn parallels with the community spirit evoked during lockdown with Britain's wartime spirit – whether you agree with this or not, 2020 has seen a resurgence in communities pulling together. Issues that previously divided us have also been put into some perspective – we've ceased to care as much about where our neighbour might stand on Europe and more about whether they've enough food or medicine to get them through the week. We've seen that age is no barrier to contributing or becoming a role model – from Captain Tom raising over £30 million for NHS Charities Together, or a couple of school children making PPE for key workers with their 3D printer.

Captain Tom's positive attitude– 'I do believe that the future is going to be much better' – was a much-needed antidote for the nation. It also served as a reminder that unswerving optimism, determination and humour, so often equated with the British Spirit, are tangible and valuable assets to hold dear.

MEDICAL PIONEERS

The Spanish Flu

Dr James Niven was Manchester's medical officer of health from 1894 to 1922. In that time his pioneering methods in public health helped cut the city's death rate from 24.2 per thousand to 13.8 per thousand. But the Scottish physician would become best known for the measures he introduced to tackle a strain of influenza that swept the city, and the rest of the globe, throughout 1918.

Although the first official cases of the disease were recorded in a US army camp, it soon became known as 'Spanish Flu'. Spain was the first country to report on it because it remained neutral during the war and didn't have any censorship restrictions in place.

The flu's symptoms were characterised by shivering, headache, sore throat and fever. If the disease progressed it could prove fatal. The majority of deaths were from pneumonia, but it could also cause haemorrhages in the lungs. Unlike many strains of influenza that came before, it attacked healthy adults, as well as the very young and elderly. Within two years it had killed between 20 and 40 million people across the world.

Many authorities were still focused on the ongoing war effort, not least the industrialised city of Manchester, where many munitions factories were based. Sir Arthur Newsholme, a senior health advisor to the British government, recommended that no factories or public buildings should be shut. But when Dr Niven began to analyse the figures surrounding the disease, he realised that schoolchildren were dying. The disease didn't discriminate.

At the time, Dr Niven's message sounded radical – the only way to stop the spread of the disease was to close down society as much as possible. He recommended the closure of schools and cinemas to reduce people's proximity to each other. His stance was not only radical but also unpopular. However, he was undeterred. He wrote regularly in the *Manchester Guardian* warning readers about the symptoms they needed to look out for. He distributed leaflets around the city that advised people on how to reduce the risk of becoming infected. And he outlined measures for self-isolation and gave nutritional advice to help people fight the disease. He also organised the distribution of free food, including baby milk, to combat starvation during the pandemic.

Dr Niven's methods proved successful. Although around 100,000 Mancunians contracted Spanish flu during the spring and summer of 1918, only 322 died. This was a significantly lower mortality rate compared to other cities.

Although he warned against large gatherings, thousands of people poured into the city to celebrate the Armistice on 11 November. By the end of the month, Dr Niven had recorded

383 influenza deaths in one week. However, his resolute position on preventative measures – although revolutionary at the time – had helped change the nation's attitude to public health for good.

In 1922, Dr Niven retired from public service. He suffered from depression and committed suicide on 30 September 1925.

DUNCAN GUTHRIE

Duncan Guthrie was a charity organiser whose commitment to fundraising for medical research improved the health and welfare of children throughout the world and many marginalised groups in society.

Duncan was born in London in 1911. At the outbreak of World War II he was assigned to the International Finnish Brigade and went on to work with the French Resistance in the Special Operations Executive. Towards the end of the war, he was parachuted into Burma where he sheltered in a village for three weeks after breaking his ankle on the drop. After the war he married Prue Holloway and they had three children.

In 1949, his first child Janet was diagnosed with polio. At the time, it was a common viral infection that provoked fear in communities – not least because it mainly attacked children under the age of five and 1 in 200 cases could result in paralysis. The disease was all the crueller because victims were often separated from their parents during long quarantine periods.

When Janet was diagnosed there was no effective vaccine. While progress was being made in the USA, some argued that it was hindered due to ignorance and fear surrounding the disease. In 1952, Duncan founded the National Fund for

Poliomyelitis Research with the aim of eradicating polio. The charity's first headquarters was just two tiny rooms above a fruit shop in Westminster.

Duncan was skilled at creating high-profile stunts that would attract the media's attention. One time he brought a real-life seal to a fundraising event at the Waldorf Hotel to introduce the popular Christmas Seals – adhesive seal stamps. He sought advice from carefully selected experts on the most effective projects to invest in. In the early days, the charity allocated funds to the first European trials of oral polio vaccines in Belfast, which went on to successfully eradicate new cases of the disease in the UK.

Duncan had achieved what he'd set out to do. However, he decided not to disband the charity and continued to fund medical research into disabling diseases. As well as funding thirteen medical chairs in universities in the UK, he began to fund technologies that would assist in the rehabilitation of paralysed people in the developing world. The fund continued to help fund research into several medical breakthroughs that included the discovery of the importance of folic acid in preventing spina bifida.

Today, the organisation is called Action Medical Research. It continues to fund medical research that will develop treatments, vaccinations and cures for many childhood diseases. Duncan Guthrie died in 1994.

Flora Murray and Louisa Garrett Anderson were both qualified doctors when their paths crossed for the first time. Before World War I, both were politically active in the suffragette movement – Louisa was briefly imprisoned for throwing a brick through a window, while Flora treated hunger-strikers released from prison and campaigned against the force-feeding of prisoners.

But for the two doctors, the battle to redress equality between the sexes was eventually fought on the wards and operating tables of their hospital at Endell Street, where any lingering taboos surrounding female doctors treating men vanished. By the end of the war, the establishment's perception of these women as enemies of the state would switch to heroes whose pioneering medical methods had saved thousands of lives. Their hospital would go down in history as the only British army hospital to be staffed and run entirely by women.

Flora and Louisa had already used their medical training to help and support people in the years running up to the outbreak of war. In 1912, they founded the Women's Hospital for Children near Paddington in London. It provided health care for working-class children in the area and gave women an opportunity to gain clinical experience in Paediatrics.

When war broke out in 1914, they founded the Women's Hospital Corps (WHC) and offered to help the French Red Cross because they believed the British War Office would reject their offer of help. The French gave them space in a newly built hotel in Paris to treat wounded patients. Flora was appointed chief physician and Louisa chief surgeon. The British War Office was extremely impressed with the success of their hospital in France and asked them to return to London to run a large military hospital. Between them they turned a former workhouse in Covent Garden into a 573-bed hospital – the Endell Street Military Hospital (ESMH). It was run entirely by an all-female team of doctors and nurses.

Louise and Flora spearheaded new techniques that focused on the psychological healing of the wounded as well as the physical. The wards were decorated with fresh flowers, and soldiers were taught needlework and taken on outings. The hospital also contained a library of more than 5,000 books.

Between May 1915 and September 1919, ESMH treated 50,000 soldiers with injuries the medical profession had never seen before. New weapons such as the machine gun presented fresh challenges for the doctors and their team who had to quickly develop new treatments that would limit infection, heal septic wounds and reduce the need for amputation. A number of their findings were published in medical journal *The Lancet*.

However, the hospital closed in 1919. As the men returned from war, attitudes towards women working in medicine – and indeed, many other professions – seemed to regress almost overnight. Women army doctors were refused equal military rank and female medical students were barred from hospitals on the grounds of modesty.

After the war, Flora and Louisa returned to work at their children's hospital in Harrow Road. However, a lack of funding led to the closure of this hospital too. They both retired and moved to a cottage in Buckinghamshire. Flora died from cancer in 1923. Louise died twenty years later at the age of seventy. They are buried together in a church near Buckinghamshire. The inscription on their gravestone reads: 'We have been gloriously happy.'

The hospital on Endell Street no longer exists but there is a plaque commemorating the work of the doctors and their all-women staff at the site today.

PIONEERING SUFFRAGETTES

SUFFRAGETTES

Regarded as one of the most important political activists in British history, Emmeline Pankhurst founded the Women's Social and Political Union (WSPU) – better known as the suffragette movement – in 1903. Her militant acts of protest alienated some supporters of the movement – including her own daughter – and to this their justification is a subject of debate. But her lifelong dedication to helping women win the right to vote for the first time and her courage in trying to achieve it is undeniable.

Born in 1858 in the Moss Side area of Manchester, Emmeline was politically active from a young age. At the age of twenty-one she married Richard Pankhurst, a barrister who advocated women's suffrage. Although they went on to have five children, Emmeline was determined to still devote time to political activities.

In the early 1890s, she met and befriended Keir Hardie and joined the Independent Labour Party (ILP), although she was initially refused membership by the local branch on account of her sex. She soon found her voice in the party and established herself as a formidable force who wanted to right every political and social wrong in society. While working as a Poor Law Guardian, she was shocked at the harsh conditions she encountered in Manchester's workhouses and immediately began to push for reforms.

However, she grew frustrated with the ILP's reluctance to make women's suffrage a priority. In 1903, she left the party and founded the WSPU. 'Deeds, not words' became their motto. In 1905, the group convinced the Liberal MP Bamford Slack to introduce a women's suffrage bill. It was ultimately obstructed, but their loud protest outside parliament attracted public attention and new supporters.

In 1906, an envoy of 300 women, representing over 125,000 suffragettes, demonstrated outside parliament. Although the then Prime Minister, Sir Henry Campbell-Bannerman, agreed in principle by their cause there was no sense of urgency within the government to hasten its progress.

The party was extremely frustrated by the lack of action taken by those in power. Many of the women in the movement had been campaigning for nearly fifty years. As a result, their tactics grew increasingly militant – from smashing windows in prominent buildings to setting unoccupied houses and churches on fire. If caught, they were imprisoned, but continued to protest by going on hunger strikes. Many of the women were force-fed, which involved strapping them down and forcing a tube through a nostril or down their throat. This practice prompted outrage from some members of the public and helped attract support for the suffragettes' cause.

The party continued to struggle with internal divisions as their tactics became even more militant and inflammatory. In 1913, several prominent figures left the WSPU, including Emmeline's two daughters, Adela and Sylvia. With the outbreak of World War I, Emmeline called a halt to the party's activism and urged women to contribute to industries that supported the British government and the war effort.

In 1916, Lloyd George, who supported women's suffrage, replaced Harold Asquith as Prime Minister. In 1918, the People's Representation Act was passed. It granted suffrage to all men over twenty-one, and for the first time, gave women, who were over the age of thirty and owned property, the right to vote. This accounted for just two-thirds of the female population.

In 1927, Emmeline was selected as the Conservative candidate for Whitechapel and St George's. However, she died in 1928 at the age of sixty-nine, just weeks before the Conservative government extended the vote to all women over the age of twenty-one. She was commemorated two years later with a statue in Victoria Tower Gardens, next to the Houses of Parliament.

In 1999, *Time* magazine named her as one of the 100 Most Important People of the 20th Century, stating that 'she shaped an idea of women for our time' and 'shook society into a new pattern from which there could be no going back'.

IN 1999, *TIME* MAGAZINE NAMED HER AS ONE OF THE 100 MOST IMPORTANT PEOPLE OF THE 20TH CENTURY

EMILY DAVISON

Emily Davison joined the WSPU in 1906. During that time she was arrested nine times, went on hunger strike seven times and was force-fed on forty-nine occasions. She died after she walked out onto the track in front of King George V's horse at the 1913 Derby.

She was born in 1872 and studied at Oxford University towards the turn of the century. She achieved first-class honours in her final exams in English but couldn't graduate because degrees from Oxford were closed to women. She went on to work as a teacher and governess before joining the suffragettes.

Emily was an officer of the organisation and a chief steward during marches. She became well known for being one of the 'most daring' of the militants. After breaking a window at a political meeting, she went on to write in the *Manchester Guardian* that this was justified because of the 'unconstitutional action of Cabinet Ministers in addressing "public meetings" from which a large section of the public were excluded' – the assembly, which was called to protest at the 1909 budget, was only open to men.

In 1911 tens of thousands of women boycotted the 1911 census by refusing to complete their census form or spoiling it with statements that included: 'No Vote, No Census' and 'I don't count, so I won't be counted'. On the night of the census Emily hid overnight in the Palace of Westminster in protest. She also successfully sued the prison authorities for using a fire hose on her during a hunger strike. Following one forced feeding she tried to commit suicide by throwing herself from one of the interior balconies of the prison, demonstrating just how far she was prepared to go in her activism. Emily believed that 'one big tragedy may save many others' from 'hideous torture'.

After one of her releases from prison she wrote in a letter to *Votes for Women*, the WSPU's newspaper: 'Through my humble work in this noblest of all causes I have come into a fullness of job and an interest in living which I never before experienced.'

On 4 June 1913, Emily travelled by train to Epsom in Surrey to attend the Derby. She carried two suffragette flags in her bag.

As the horses approached the home straight, she stood in wait on the final bend before stepping out in front of Anmer, a horse belonging to the king. She was knocked to the ground unconscious and died from her injuries four days later in hospital. There are still questions surrounding whether or not Emily intended to kill herself, as she never discussed her plans with anyone. Some historians argue she was trying to pin one of the suffragette banners to the horse, which is an explanation that has been corroborated by forensic examiners. At the time, the verdict of the inquest was 'death by misadventure'.

On 14 June 1913, Emily's body was carried from Epsom to London. Her coffin was inscribed: 'Fight on. God will give the victory'. 5,000 women and hundreds of male supporters formed a procession. Her gravestone bears the WSPU slogan 'Deeds, not words'.

In 1990, the Labour MPs Tony Benn and Jeremy Corbyn placed a commemorative plaque inside the cupboard where Emily had hidden during the census eighty years earlier. In April 2013, a plaque was unveiled at Epsom racecourse to mark the centenary of her death.

EDITH MARGARET GARRUD

In 1913, the Asquith government passed the Prisoners (Temporary Discharge for Ill Health) Act. It was more commonly known as the 'Cat and Mouse Act'.

This allowed the authorities to release suffragettes who were close to death due to malnourishment. However, they could be re-imprisoned on their original charges once they were healthy again. This was an attempt to avoid force-feeding. In response, the WSPU established an all-women protection unit known as The Bodyguard, to protect suffragettes from re-arrest and at demonstrations where they would often be assaulted by police and also by male bystanders. They were trained in self-defence techniques – specifically jiu-jitsu – by Edith Margaret Garrud, the first female professional martial arts instructor in the Western world. The lessons took place in secret.

Edith and her husband William were introduced to jiu-jitsu by Edward William Barton-Wright in 1899. By 1908, Edith was teaching classes to women and children at a jiu-jitsu school in Soho, London. Soon after, she began teaching self-defence to selected members of the suffragettes who were tasked with protecting the movement's leaders.

Edith also taught other techniques to the women, such as disguise and decoy, in order to escape arrest. One night in early 1914, Emmeline Pankhurst addressed a large crowd from a balcony in Camden Square where she challenged the police to re-arrest her – at that point she was a fugitive under the Cat and Mouse Act. A few minutes later she emerged outside the front of the house, escorted by members of The Bodyguard. As the police swept in to arrest her, a short fight ensued. But by the time they'd knocked their target to the ground and carried her away to a nearby station, the real Emmeline had already escaped from another exit.

Emmeline Pankhurst's personal bodyguard, Leonora Cohen, earned the title 'Tower Suffragette' when she smashed the display case for the Crown Jewels in the Tower of London. Leonora lived until she was 105 and protested with feminists into the 1970s.

Edith and William continued to work as self-defence and jiu-jitsu instructors until 1925. There was renewed interest in Edith's work with the suffragettes in the 1960s and a number of docudramas have been made about her. She died in 1971, aged ninety-nine.

THEY WERE TRAINED IN SELF-DEFENCE TECHNIQUES – SPECIFICALLY JIU-JITSU – BY EDITH MARGARET GARRUD, THE FIRST FEMALE PROFESSIONAL MARTIAL ARTS INSTRUCTOR IN THE WESTERN WORLD. THE LESSONS TOOK PLACE IN SECRET.

MILLICENT FAWCETT

Millicent Fawcett once wrote: 'I cannot say I became a suffragist. I always was one, from the time I was old enough to think at all about the principles of Representative Government.'

Her fundamental belief in equality for women informed everything that she campaigned for throughout her life – from improving women's access to education – she was a co-founder of Newnham College, Cambridge, in 1871– to leading Britain's largest women's rights organisation, the National Union of Women's Suffrage Societies (NUWSS).

In 2018, 100 years after the passing of the Representation of the People Act, Millicent became the first woman to be commemorated with a statue in Parliament Square. It's surprising, perhaps, that it took so long.

Millicent was born in 1847, at a time when everything a woman owned belonged to a man, including themselves. In total, Millicent dedicated sixty-two years of her life to campaigning for women's rights. She began in 1866, at the age of nineteen, when she collected signatures for a petition for the right for women to vote. She set up the first suffrage society in 1867 and travelled the country to speak at public meetings. Millicent was just twenty-two when she undertook her first speaking tour, at a time when women rarely even spoke in public.

In 1897, she brought all suffrage societies together under the NUWSS. By 1907 it had tens of thousands of members. She went on to establish the International Women's Suffrage Alliance, which linked up with campaigners from all over the world.

Millicent was also particularly passionate about the rights of working-class women and enabled them to be actively involved in the movement. She also campaigned against child labour and child sex abuse. She fought for equal access for women to divorce and wrote the introduction to the re-published *A Vindication of the Rights of Woman* by Mary Wollstonecraft in 1891. As well, Millicent campaigned to repeal the Contagious Diseases Acts that reflected unfair societal double standards and required prostitutes to be examined for sexually transmitted diseases. If they were found to have passed disease to their clients, they were imprisoned.

She was determined to keep strictly to the principle of supporting the suffrage movement through argument alone and distanced herself from the militant actions of the WPSU. As the WPSU ceased their activities at the outbreak of war, the NUWSS continued to campaign, highlighting the contribution that women made to the war effort. She held her post until 1919, a year after the first women were granted the vote.

In the 1925 New Year Honours she was appointed Dame Grand Cross of the Order of the British Empire (GBE). She died in 1929.

In 1932, a memorial to Millicent, alongside that of her husband, was unveiled in Westminster Abbey. Today the Fawcett Society continues to campaign for gender equality and women's rights at work, at home and in public life.

MILLICENT WAS JUST TWENTY-TWO WHEN SHE UNDERTOOK HER FIRST SPEAKING TOUR, AT A TIME WHEN WOMEN RARELY EVEN SPOKE IN PUBLIC.

HEROES OF WAR

WW1

William Walker from Kennington in south London learnt to master the bugle as a young boy when he joined the Boys' Brigade in 1912. In May 1916, he took up the position of bugler, on board the HMS *Calliope*. He was just sixteen.

The ship was one of 151 British warships that were pitted against the Germans during the Battle of Jutland. It was one of the largest sea battles of World War I and lasted for two days. 'Young Bill', as he became known, stood with the captain to sound the 'Commence' – a bugle call that signalled the start of battle.

William remained at his post while the ship fought back against a torpedo attack from the Germans. During the battle the ship was hit three times and a dozen men were killed. That day, a splinter from a shell struck William and wounded him severely. But the young man refused to leave his captain's side until he fainted from a loss of blood.

He was taken to RNQ hospital in Scotland, where he was

treated for his wounds. While he recovered there, news of his bravery spread and he even received a visit from King George V while recovering in hospital. When he arrived home on leave, he was surprised to find he'd been dubbed the 'Kennington hero'. But the honour that 'Young Bill' treasured most dearly was the recognition of his heroism. In October 1916 Royal Navy Officer Admiral Sir John Jellicoe presented him with a specially inscribed bugle to commemorate his bravery.

ARTHUR POULTER

Arthur Poulter was a twenty-four-year-old private in the British Army in World War I. He was awarded the Victoria Cross for bravely carrying wounded soldiers to safety under enemy fire during the Battle of Lys.

Born in East Witton, north Yorkshire in 1893, Arthur was one of nine sons who all served in the war. At the age of nineteen he moved to Leeds where he worked as drayman and subsequently a cartman. In 1916 he married Ada Briggs. In the same year he enlisted with the Duke of Wellington's (West Riding) Regiment, British Army during World War I.

In the spring of 1918, the German Army launched Operation Georgette. They massed thirty-six divisions in Flanders, east of the French town of Armentières with the objective of capturing Ypres and forcing the British back to the Channel ports. On 10 April 1918, they broke through the brigade that were holding the line in the town of Erquinghem-Lys, which had been held by the British since 1914.

Orders to evacuate Armentières and to withdraw over

the river Lys were issued in the morning. But by the time they were received, the regiment was already under fierce attacks from the German army in Erquinghem-Lys, northern France. Arthur's regiment found themselves surrounded by the enemy with few routes of escape as many of the town's bridges had been destroyed.

Arthur was one of the stretcher-bearers, who found himself caught in the crossfire as he carried wounded soldiers to safety, the casualties mounting drastically. Before long, all of the stretcher-bearers in the regiment had been killed or wounded and Arthur was the only one left. He made ten separate trips facing a barrage of artillery, machine gun fire and hailing shrapnel each time, carrying the wounded soldiers for 500 yards over the river to the Royal Army Medical Corps. At one point, he carried two men on his back and even managed to bandage forty men while under fire.

Arthur was presented with the Victoria Cross at Buckingham Palace in December 1918 for his bravery during the battle. However, he had been seriously wounded and spent the remainder of the war in various military hospitals. He went on to have eight children with his wife and work for the Leeds Transport Depot.

In June 1999, the Poulter family decided to donate Arthur's VC to the Duke of Wellington's Regiment Museum in Halifax, Yorkshire.

AT ONE POINT, HE CARRIED TWO MEN ON HIS BACK AND EVEN MANAGED TO BANDAGE FORTY MEN WHILE UNDER FIRE.

EDITH CAVELL

The inscription on Edith Cavell's memorial near Trafalgar Square reads: 'Patriotism is not enough; I must have no hatred or bitterness for anyone.' These words were spoken by the British nurse to an Anglican priest the night before her death. Although it seems difficult to believe she could have been this forgiving towards the German firing squad who executed her the following morning, this was a woman who remained determined to show kindness and humanity to everyone – regardless of the side they fought on – to the very end.

Edith was born in Norfolk, in 1865. A governess before she trained to be a nurse in London, she worked in hospitals throughout the capital and Manchester before accepting a position as matron at the Berkendael Medical institute in Brussels. At the time, there was no established nursing profession in Belgium when Edith was appointed. Her pioneering methods helped transform modern nursing education in that country.

In the summer of 1914, she was in Norfolk visiting her mother when war broke out. Although German troops were advancing on the city, she felt compelled to return to the hospital immediately.

By the end of August, Brussels was occupied by the Germans and Berkendael had become a Red Cross hospital. Edith encouraged the nurses to treat any soldiers that came through their doors, regardless of which side they were fighting on.

Following the Battle of Mons – the first battle in which British forces clashed with German soldiers on the French borders – Edith treated two wounded British men in the hospital. She then arranged to have them smuggled out of the country into the neutral Netherlands.

Over the next year she became part of a network of people that helped around 200 British, French and Belgian soldiers. She risked her life sheltering them in the hospital until they were well, smuggling them out through an underground passage and providing them with money and false identity cards, organising guides to help them get to the border. Although she aroused suspicion from the German authorities and was advised to flee by the British, she insisted on continuing to help.

On 5 August 1915, the secret tunnel beneath the hospital was uncovered. She was arrested by the Germans and placed in solitary confinement in St Gilles Prison in Brussels. When she was interrogated she chose not to lie and confessed.

In October, Edith was tried at court martial along with thirty-four other people who'd been connected to the network. Although an international outcry ensued and the world clamoured for her release, she was shot by a firing squad on 12 October 1915.

Her execution caused outrage in Britain and in many neutral countries across the world, including the United States. After the war, her bravery was honoured in a memorial service that was held at Westminster Abbey.

In 1920, a ten-foot sculpture of Edith in her nursing uniform was erected in St Martin's Place near Trafalgar Square. It still stands today as a memorial to her. She is buried in Norwich Cathedral.

COURAGEOUS CAMPAIGNERS

EDWARD BIRCHILL

Edward Birchall was a philanthropist who left a legacy of £1000 in 1916 to promote voluntary services in the UK. This led to the formation of the National Council of Social Services, which later became the National Council for Voluntary Organisations (NCVO).

Edward was born in 1884 in Upton St Leonards, Gloucestershire. From an early age he demonstrated an altruistic nature and in 1911 he founded the Agenda Club, which embodied the values of a burgeoning movement that aimed to make social work more inclusive, community-based, and less reliant on the state.

He served as secretary on the newly formed National Association of Guilds of Help and the Charity Organisation Society, which set up projects for the sick, children and the unemployed. He was also a civil servant, employed in the labour exchanges and unemployment insurance department of the Board of Trade. It was here that he became friends with Percy Grundy, general secretary of the Manchester League of Help. Together they created a vision of an organisation that brought together the Guilds of Help, the Charitable Organisation Society and the councils of social welfare.

But when war broke out in 1914, Edward became a captain in the infantry in the British Army. There was a surge of voluntary activity in World War I as thousands of new organisations sprang up across the country to help alleviate the suffering. Edward and his peers recognised the need for a body that would connect and represent them.

A year later, Edward was still on the front line and feared his own death might be imminent. He wrote to his friend Percy and bequeathed him £1000, to support their vision of a unified organisation. In 1916, Edward died during the Battle of the Somme, while heading his regiment into battle. He was awarded a posthumous Distinguished Order.

Percy went on to fulfil Edward's wish. In 1919, he set up the National Council of Social Services (NCSS) with other philanthropists who honoured the core values at the heart of the new philanthropy movement.

The NCSS paved the way for many different charitable organisations – Age Concern (now Age UK), Citizens Advice, and the Charities Aid Foundation. Today, its name has changed to the National Council of Voluntary Organisations and it continues to champion and support the voluntary sector and volunteering today.

CLAUDIA JONES

Claudia Jones was born in 1915 in Belmont, Port of Spain, Trinidad and Tobago. She emigrated to New York with her family in 1924, following the post-war cocoa price crash.

From an early age, she was fully aware of the damage that inequality inflicted. As a teenager she contracted tuberculosis due to poor living conditions. The disease would plague her health for subsequent decades and eventually contribute to her early death. She was a brilliant student who excelled at school academically, but her family were so poor they couldn't afford to go to her graduation.

Although Claudia had lived in New York since she was nine, she was classed as an immigrant, which significantly limited her career choices. At this time she began to look for ways to express herself politically, speaking out against racism, sexism and class oppression in her column 'Claudia Comments' for a Harlem journal.

In 1936 she joined the Young Communist League in support of their campaign to save the lives of, and free, the 'Scottsboro Boys' – a group of nine young African-American men who faced execution in Alabama after they were falsely accused of raping a white woman.

Although she was an active member of the organisation, she was also a vocal critic of their failure to acknowledge challenges that limited opportunities for black and white women to find work and fully engage in activism. Claudia argued for equal pay, theoretical training and childcare programmes.

An avid writer and journalist who believed in the power of words, she wrote articles that merged Marxist theories with the oppression of black women in society. One of her best-known pieces of writing is 'An End to the Neglect of the Problems of the Negro Woman!' which appeared in the magazine *Political Affairs* in 1949.

As anti-communist feelings gathered pace across the country, Claudia was arrested, sentenced to prison and threatened with deportation. In 1951 she was convicted for 'un-American activities' against the government. However, she was refused entrance to Trinidad and Tobago, in part because the authorities thought she might 'prove troublesome'.

Claudia was eventually offered residency in the UK on humanitarian grounds. When she arrived in London at the end of 1955, it was commonplace to find signs on rental properties, shops and even some government establishments that said: 'No Irish, No Coloured, No Dogs'. The British African-Caribbean community was expanding in west London but Claudia found that they lacked a proper political power base. She brought together a network of people within the community that campaigned for equal rights in housing, education and employment. She also fought against the Commonwealth Immigrants Bill – which made it harder for non-Whites to migrate to Britain – and campaigned for the release of Nelson Mandela.

Claudia believed that 'people without a voice were as lambs to the slaughter'. In March 1958, she founded the anti-racist and anti-imperialist paper, *West Indian Gazette*, which helped to unite and unify voices within the Black British community.

Four months after the launch of the paper, an increase in violent attacks against the black community resulted in the Notting Hill race riots. In the aftermath, Claudia suggested that the community should hold a Mardi Gras-based carnival as a positive response to the riots.

In January 1959, she organised a carnival in St Pancras Town Hall – the Boscoe Holder dance troupe, jazz guitarist Fitzroy Coleman and singer Cleo Laine all headlined. The event was televised nationally by the BBC and is widely acknowledged as a precursor to the famous Notting Hill carnival that takes place each year in the summer.

Claudia died in January 1965, at the age of forty-nine. She is buried near the tomb of her hero Karl Marx in Highgate Cemetery, London.

MAX LEVITAS

The year was 1934. While the British Union of Fascists (BUF) continued to attract support across the country, a young Jewish, Irish-born activist from the East End of London headed for Trafalgar Square one night in early September to protest. Along with his friend he painted a series of anti-Fascist slogans in whitewash across Nelson's Column.

It was the first time Max Levitas protested against Fascism, but it certainly wouldn't be the last. Two years later he took part in the 'Battle of Cable Street' in the East End – now regarded as one of the most extraordinary examples in British history of what can be achieved through social solidarity. Max, along with 300,000 people, formed a human chain that prevented Oswald Mosley – the leader of the British Union of Fascists – and 3,000 Blackshirts from marching through the community, where a large number of Jewish people lived and worked. It was incredible for the young Max to witness what ordinary people could achieve when they united.

With the outbreak of World War II, the UK's citizens were encouraged to unite against a common enemy – fascism. But Max, an active member of the Stepney Young Communist League, could see there were still many divisions and inequalities across society that needed to be addressed. At the beginning of the war he served as a fire warden in the East End. As the Germans launched a series of devastating attacks against civilians in the capital, Max saw first-hand the vulnerability of people who lived in the more impoverished parts of the East End.

The majority relied on surface or trench shelters, which would protect them from little else but shrapnel or flak. These soon filled up with water and were useless in the event of a direct hit from attacking aircraft. In contrast to the inadequate shelter provisions found in the East End, people who lived in wealthier areas of the capital benefitted from far more extensive preparations.

East Enders joked in the early days of the Blitz that they had learnt to 'hug the walls' when they were caught out during a raid. But it was no laughing matter and Max knew that action had to be taken to save lives.

He, with fellow members of the Communist Party, argued for deeper air raid shelters and better provision in the East End. But the request was largely ignored by the government. At this point they were still refusing to open up the underground for civilians.

On 14 September 1940 – the eighth night of the Blitz in London – Max gathered at the foot of the Embankment with around forty other protesters. Some included the members of the Stepney Tenants' Defence League – who'd organised rent strikes against slum landlords in the 1930s. From there, they marched to the lobby of the nearby Savoy Hotel on the Strand. They had heard reports that a well-constructed and luxurious shelter had been built for guests of the hotel.

Within minutes, they occupied the underground bomb shelter beneath the Savoy, meeting with little opposition from the management who were reluctant to turf them out during an air raid. Years later, Max said of the event: 'It was easy for the government to ignore our message sitting in the basement of a very nice hotel. So we decided to march on one.'

The demonstration made headlines all over the world and highlighted the unfair disparities between conditions in the shelters of the East End and West London. It inspired similar protests in other parts of the capital.

As a result, the government made moves to improve the shelters in the East End and announced they would open up the underground stations for shelter. They also agreed to install bunks and provide refreshments and first aid.

After the war, Max went on to become a councillor for Tower Hamlets London Borough Council for fifteen years. He continued to live in the East End and remained an active campaigner in local housing and pensioners' groups. In 2013, he spoke at a rally in opposition of the English Defence League. He died in 2018, aged 103.

**MAX, ALONG WITH 300,000 PEOPLE, FORMED
A HUMAN CHAIN THAT PREVENTED OSWALD
MOSLEY – THE LEADER OF THE BRITISH UNION
OF FASCISTS – AND 3,000 BLACKSHIRTS FROM
MARCHING THROUGH THE COMMUNITY, WHERE
A LARGE NUMBER OF JEWISH PEOPLE LIVED
AND WORKED.**

CANON NORMAN POWER

As a child, Norman Power witnessed the impact of social injustice growing up in Newcastle-on-Tyne, where his father was vicar in a poverty-stricken parish. But he also saw how people banded together to support each other in communities. In 1926, Norman's family moved to Birmingham. He moved away to study, but returned to the city when he was ordained a priest in 1940.

After the war, Birmingham's council authorities vowed to sweep the city of its decrepit housing and slums to make way for American-style high rises. But Norman could foresee just how problematic this could be for some of Birmingham's poorest and isolated families. He resolved to speak up for the most isolated communities, who were also at risk of being swept away in Birmingham's post-war utopian vision.

In the early 1950s, Norman moved to St John's Church in Ladywood, an inner city district. At the time, redevelopment was in full swing. Norman agreed that the authorities needed to destroy bad housing. But he believed they should be replaced with homes rather than tower blocks, which would separate people from their communities. He also objected to the exile of local people, many of whom were relocated to live in new towns or estates. He argued they should be allowed to rent new properties in their own neighbourhoods and preserve their communities. Norman was also one of the first people to predict and identify the tensions that could arise from class segregation.

Norman put his ideas forward in a weekly column in the *Birmingham Evening Mail* and his book, *The Forgotten People*, which was published in 1965. But sadly, his pleas to preserve communities were largely ignored. In the years following the city's transformation, many of the regenerated areas became forgotten wastelands. However, Norman's efforts were not entirely in vain. His ideas found new ground and inspired other people of faith to start a housing movement that aimed to put people at the centre of decisions.

Norman never deserted the area and remained committed to improving Ladywood for the communities that remained there. From the early 1950s, he and his wife organised a weekly camp for local children every summer. Despite his own financial hardships he worked hard to find the funds and kept the annual trip going for twenty-five years.

In 1988, Norman retired from his ministry. He died in 1993. He is still remembered incredibly fondly by the people of Ladywood and there has been reignited interest in his book *The Forgotten People* in recent years. In 2013, twenty years after his death, a reunion was held in his honour at St John's Church, to commemorate his memory.

EGLANTYNE JEBB

Eglantyne Jebb was a social reformer who believed that every single child across the world deserved the chance of a happy and fulfilling childhood, no matter the background or country they were born into. Towards the end of World War I, she began a campaign to raise awareness of starving children in Europe that laid the foundations for the international charity Save The Children and The Declaration of the Rights of the Child.

Eglantyne was born in 1876, in Shropshire, to a wealthy family of philanthropists who believed in social justice and education. She studied History at Oxford and trained as a schoolteacher. She decided not to pursue teaching as a career, but her experiences opened her eyes to the challenges of poverty that many children faced in society.

She moved to Cambridge where she became involved in the Charity Organisation Society. She carried out extensive research on social issues affecting the city and in 1906 she published a book, *Cambridge, a Study in Social Questions*, based on her findings. The following year she was appointed to the Education Committee of Cambridge Borough Council. In 1913 she travelled to Macedonia on behalf of the Macedonian Relief Fund.

During World War I Eglantyne became involved in a project with her sister Dorothy that highlighted the impact of the war on children in enemy countries Austria and Germany. They were shocked to discover that many were starving due to the Allied blockade, which stopped food and medical supplies getting through and continued even after the Armistice.

In 1919 she joined a group Fight the Famine Council to put pressure on the government to end the blockade. One day she was arrested in Trafalgar Square for handing out leaflets that showed pictures of starving children with the headline: 'Our blockade has caused this – millions of children are starving to death.' She was found guilty and fined for protesting. However, the judge was moved by her commitment to children's rights and paid her fine.

In 1919, Fight the Famine Council set up a fund to raise money for the children. The British public responded generously and volunteers were dispatched to organise relief work. Their fundraising success inspired Eglantyne and Dorothy to set up the International Save the Children Union in Geneva. Eglantyne took charge of the organisation and began to raise substantial amounts of money through some fairly novel methods – these included full-page adverts in national papers and films that were screened in local cinemas, which showed footage of the conditions children faced. By 1921 the situation in Europe had improved. However, there was a bigger emergency further east, as the people of Soviet Russia faced a famine.

In the autumn of 1921, Save the Children sent a cargo ship carrying 600 tons of food and medical supplies to Russia to be distributed – it was a move that helped to keep 300,000 children and more than 350,000 adults alive.

Save the Children had never been set up as a permanent organisation but, as it dealt with emergency after emergency, it soon became known as an effective relief agency.

As peace returned to Europe, Save the Children focused its attention on children's rights. In 1923, Eglantyne headed to Geneva for a meeting with the International Union to plan a Children's Charter. From this she drafted a document that outlined the duty of the international community to put children's rights at the heart and centre of their planning. A year later, The Declaration of the Rights of the Child, or the Declaration of Geneva as it came to be known, was adopted by the League of Nations.

In 1925, the first International Child Welfare congress was held in Geneva, where the declaration was supported by organisations and governments. An updated version was adopted by the United Nations in 1959, and it was the influence behind the 1989 UN Convention on the Rights of the Child over sixty years later.

In 1928, Eglantyne died in a nursing home in Geneva, after suffering years of ill health due to a thyroid problem.

Today, Save the Children continues to fight for a world where every child has the chance to live their life free from disease, starvation and fear.

FROM THIS SHE DRAFTED A DOCUMENT THAT OUTLINED THE DUTY OF THE INTERNATIONAL COMMUNITY TO PUT CHILDREN'S RIGHTS AT THE HEART AND CENTRE OF THEIR PLANNING. A YEAR LATER, THE DECLARATION OF THE RIGHTS OF THE CHILD, OR THE DECLARATION OF GENEVA AS IT CAME TO BE KNOWN, WAS ADOPTED BY THE LEAGUE OF NATIONS.

PIONEERING
WOMEN

WWII

WAAFS

'The Battle of Britain' is synonymous with Spitfire pilots bravely battling Messerschmitts high above the skies of England. But its victory didn't take place in the air alone. The individual actions of people on the ground also contributed greatly to the RAF's eventual defeat of the Luftwaffe.

On 1 September 1940, three servicewomen reported for duty at Biggin Hill, a Royal Air Force station in Kent. Sergeant Joan Mortimer, Corporal Elspeth Henderson and Sergeant Helen Turner worked as teleprinter operators in the Sector Operations Room – or 'the hole' – as it was known at Biggin Hill.

They were just three of several thousand young women who had joined the Women's Auxiliary Air Force (WAAF), during the summer of 1940. Many of them played a key role in helping to operate the radar system, which directed aircraft and anti-artillery aircraft against enemy targets.

The airfield, which was one of the most important fighter bases during the Battle of Britain, had suffered five separate raids over the previous two days.

On 30 August, a dozen bombers had destroyed workshops, barracks and one of the last remaining hangars: thirty-nine people were killed. On 31 August, the Germans mounted a larger operation that wreaked even more havoc on the airfield. Incredibly, it was up and running again the following day. But after two days of sustained attacks, the women knew there was no reason to believe the Germans wouldn't return again for a sixth raid. They were right. That day the Luftwaffe raided the airfield twice.

During their second attack, a 500-pound bomb was dropped on the sector operations room, partially destroying the defence teleprinter network. Although Elspeth was knocked to the ground she maintained contact with Fighter Command Headquarters in Uxbridge throughout the raid, while Helen continued to operate the switchboard, communicating with squadron dispersal points.

Joan was working in the armoury when the air raid started. Although she was surrounded by high explosives, she stayed at her position at the telephone switchboard and continued to communicate with defence posts around the airfield. Joan also went outside to mark the areas where bombs lay unexploded, even as one exploded nearby. Elspeth and Helen only left their posts when they were ordered to because the building was on fire.

Biggin Hill suffered a further six raids. However, it remained operational throughout the entire period of the Battle of the Britain. There was only one week when the damage was so severe that only one squadron could operate from it.

In November 1940, each of the three servicewomen were awarded a Military Medal for their determination to carry out their duties, under difficult and dangerous conditions.

JOAN ALSO WENT OUTSIDE TO MARK THE AREAS WHERE BOMBS LAY UNEXPLODED, EVEN AS ONE EXPLODED NEARBY. ELSPETH AND HELEN ONLY LEFT THEIR POSTS WHEN THEY WERE ORDERED TO BECAUSE THE BUILDING WAS ON FIRE.

LILIAN BADER

During World War II Lilian Bader became one of the very first black women to join the British Armed Forces. Throughout her life she'd faced prejudice, discrimination and hardship. Despite this, she went on to successfully rise through the ranks in the Women's Auxiliary Air Force (WAAF).

Lilian was born in 1918 in the Toxteth Park area of Liverpool. Her father Marcus Bailey was a Barbadian-born migrant who served in the Royal Navy as a merchant seaman. Her mother Lilian McGowan was of Irish parentage.

In 1927, Lilian was nine when she and her two older brothers were orphaned, due to circumstances that remain unclear. The trio were separated and Lilian was placed in a convent. She was a bright and personable student. However, no one was willing to employ her so she remained in the convent till the age of twenty.

Eventually, she found work in domestic service. Then war broke out in 1939. Lilian joined the Navy, Army and Air

Force Institutes (NAAFI) at Catterick Camp, Yorkshire as a canteen assistant. She was enjoying her new role but within seven weeks she was asked to leave – an official in London had discovered her father was born outside the UK.

Lilian found work again in January 1940 on a farm near RAF Topcliffe, where she met soldiers who ventured from the base. One day she heard some West Indians being interviewed on the radio. She was intrigued to hear that although they'd been turned down by the army, the RAF had accepted them.

On 28 March 1941, Lilian joined the WAAF and was sent to York, where she trained to be an instrument repairer. It was a relatively new job that had been made available to women in 1940 and involved running routine repairs and replacing sensitive equipment. Yet two weeks into her training she received devastating news: her brother who, like their father, was serving in the merchant navy had been lost at sea.

Incredibly, despite this, Lilian excelled in her exams and passed her course 'First Class', becoming one of the first women in the Air Force to qualify in that trade. She was posted to RAF Shawbury where she worked long hours checking for faults in the aircraft, going on to become a leading aircraftwoman and earning herself the rank of corporal.

In 1943, she married a mixed-race serviceman, Ramsay Bader, who was engaged in the D-Day landings. In 1944, she was discharged from the WAAF when she became pregnant with the first of their two children. Lilian went on to gain a degree from University of London and became a teacher.

In 1989, Lilian's memoir was published: *Together – Lilian Bader: Wartime Memoirs of a WAAF 1939–1944*. In 1990, she took part in a BBC2 programme with ex-servicemen and women from the former African and Caribbean colonies, where they debated the pros and cons of serving Britain in the world wars. When they received some criticism from audience members for supporting the British war effort, Lilian explained that she had joined the WAAF to ensure Britain's black citizens didn't suffer the same fate that they did in Nazi Germany and occupied Europe.

As the twentieth century neared to an end, three generations of Lilian's family had served in the British Forces. She commented: 'Father served in the First World War, his three children served in the Second World War. I married a coloured man who was in the Second World War, as was his brother who was decorated for bravery in Burma. Their father also served in the First World War. Our son was a helicopter pilot, he served in Northern Ireland. So all in all, I think we've given back more to this country than we've received.'

She died in 2015 at the age of ninety-seven.

'FATHER SERVED IN THE FIRST WORLD WAR, HIS THREE CHILDREN SERVED IN THE SECOND WORLD WAR. I MARRIED A COLOURED MAN WHO WAS IN THE SECOND WORLD WAR, AS WAS HIS BROTHER WHO WAS DECORATED FOR BRAVERY IN BURMA. THEIR FATHER ALSO SERVED IN THE FIRST WORLD WAR. OUR SON WAS A HELICOPTER PILOT, HE SERVED IN NORTHERN IRELAND. SO ALL IN ALL, I THINK WE'VE GIVEN BACK MORE TO THIS COUNTRY THAN WE'VE RECEIVED.'

SUE RYDER

Sue Ryder was born in Leeds, Yorkshire in 1923. From a young age she wanted to help other people, assisting her mother who helped people in the slums of the city. She was sixteen when World War II broke out and her experiences throughout the next six years would have a profound influence on the path she decided to take in life. Whether she was finding homes for the displaced or improving palliative care, she chose to commit her life to caring for other people and relieving their suffering.

At the outbreak of war, Sue volunteered to be a nurse with the First Aid Nursing Yeomanry (FANY). She was soon posted to the Polish section of the Special Operations Executive (SOE), where she met many Polish resistance fighters risking their lives to support the Allies.

At the end of the conflict, she volunteered for relief work in Poland, where she met survivors of Nazi atrocities. Desperate to help refugees in post-war Europe she set up the Sue Ryder homes – years later the Polish people honoured her with the title 'Lady Ryder of Warsaw'.

Sue worked tirelessly to find homes for young Poles who'd been left to languish in German prisons. Within twenty months she'd organised passes for 1400 Poles to return home. In 1952, she started a holiday scheme for those who were still in relief camps and founded a home for men who had been in prison. It was such a success she started the Sue Ryder Foundation, which built care centres across Europe for the disabled and people with terminal illnesses.

The homes were supported by a network of charity shops across Britain that sold new and second-hand items. The foundation exists to this day, continuing to support the terminally ill and providing care for people with neurological conditions. It also provides bereavement support and campaigns for improvements in palliative care.

Sue Ryder was appointed OBE in 1957. In 1979, she was made a life peer in the House of Lords. She routinely travelled 50,000 miles around the globe each year to visit people in the homes she'd set up. Her enduring love for Poland never died – when the country began to break free from communism she organised for many lorry loads of aid to be sent there. Sue died in 2000, leaving the legacy of her charitable work in many corners of the world.

AT THE END OF THE CONFLICT, SHE VOLUNTEERED FOR RELIEF WORK IN POLAND, WHERE SHE MET SURVIVORS OF NAZI ATROCITIES. DESPERATE TO HELP REFUGEES IN POST-WAR EUROPE SHE SET UP THE SUE RYDER HOMES – YEARS LATER THE POLISH PEOPLE HONOURED HER WITH THE TITLE 'LADY RYDER OF WARSAW'.

STELLA ISAACS

A journalist once said of Stella Isaacs: 'Had she been a man she would have become prime minister.' Born at the turn of the twentieth century, Stella probably came as close to realising this as any woman of her generation, with her credentials and connections, ever could. In 1958 she became the first woman to take a seat in the House of Lords. Stella had never been content to settle for what society expected of her. Nor did she shy from encouraging other women to defy society's expectations – least of all in their contribution to the war effort.

In the late 1930s, as war looked increasingly inevitable, Stella founded the Women's Voluntary Service (WVS). In one WVS recruitment poster, on which her face appears, she addresses women directly with a rallying call –'Housewives! WVS needs your help! Even if tied to your home you can help the wardens and your neighbours.' The campaign worked. By 1940, one in ten women, from more than 2000 cities, towns and villages across Britain, volunteered for the WVS to assist with civil defence tasks.

Stella was born in 1894 in, what was then, Constantinople to a large wealthy family – her father was a director of the tobacco monopoly of the Ottoman Empire. She suffered from ill health throughout her childhood and was educated by private tutors.

During World War I she volunteered as a nurse in the Voluntary Aid Detachment, although there is some evidence she was ill suited to this because she couldn't bear the sight of blood. She also began to train as a secretary in London.

In 1925, she joined the Viceroy's staff in Delhi, India, serving as secretary to Lady Reading, the wife of the Viceroy, Rufus Isaacs. She soon rose to become his chief of staff. In 1930, his wife died and Stella became his political hostess. A year later Stella and Rufus married and she became Lady Reading. At this point, Rufus was serving as foreign secretary for Ramsay MacDonald's national government.

Stella leveraged her position to campaign for the causes she cared about. In 1932 she became chair of the Personal Service League, a women's voluntary organisation that collected second-hand clothes for the unemployed. She also began to develop strong ties with America – Rufus had been British Ambassador to the US and believed better understanding between the two countries was fundamental to the future of democracy.

After his death in 1935, Stella went to the US. Her desire to alleviate poverty was genuine and she immersed herself in experiences that gave her a genuine understanding of 'ordinary' Americans' – in 1935 she worked as a dishwasher and stayed in cheap lodgings as she travelled the country. She became close friends with Eleanor Roosevelt, who shared her vision to alleviate poverty.

In 1938, Stella founded the WVS. The women volunteers came from many different socio and economic backgrounds. They were asked 'not to fight ... but to relieve suffering and to safeguard ... to build up, to repair and conserve'. The colour of their uniforms earned them the name 'the ladies in green'.

Women's duties during WWII were often viewed as homely or domestic – they knitted clothes (sometimes from dog hair) and issued children with protective masks and helmets. Some of the women turned their hands to carpentry, creating toys for children while others operated 'Blitz canteens' across London to provide refreshments to troops and civilians.

But it also provided a wide variety of training courses – from driving in the blackout to how to evacuate people from cities at risk of bombing. At the end of August 1939 the WVS helped to evacuate 1.5 million children, pregnant women and other vulnerable people from the cities to the countryside, three days before war was declared.

The women also helped to coordinate housing for more than 9000 people who were made homeless following air raids. Many of the women risked their lives as motorcycle messengers, carrying important, and often confidential, messages between WVS headquarters, government departments and other WVS centres. Meg Moorat, nicknamed Miss Mercury, was just one of those messengers.

By the end of the war, the WVS had a million members and the organisation was hailed as the 'Greatest Women's Army in the World'. Many of the initiatives that the organisation started during the war influenced future services provided by state welfare – from 'meals on wheels' to home-help support.

In 1960, the organisation sent a 1,000 tons of second-hand clothing to refugees in the Middle East. In 2013, it became the Royal Voluntary Service (RVS). Today, it continues to provide a great number of different services that support the elderly.

After the war, Stella set up Women's Home Industries, a successful company that exported clothing and craft made by home-based women to the US. In 1958, she was made a life peer in the House of Lords where she continued to speak up for the rights of refugees and displaced people.

She chaired the Home Office's Advisory Council (1962–65) that played a leading role in facilitating the Windrush migration to Britain from the Commonwealth. She also led a working party on the after-care of prisoners released from jail. Stella died in 1971.

IN 1958 SHE BECAME THE FIRST WOMAN TO TAKE A SEAT IN THE HOUSE OF LORDS. STELLA HAD NEVER BEEN CONTENT TO SETTLE FOR WHAT SOCIETY EXPECTED OF HER. NOR DID SHE SHY FROM ENCOURAGING OTHER WOMEN TO DEFY SOCIETY'S EXPECTATIONS – LEAST OF ALL IN THEIR CONTRIBUTION TO THE WAR EFFORT.

VERA LYNN

In 1939, singer Vera Lynn was voted 'Forces' Sweetheart' by British servicemen and women in a newspaper poll. But in the dark days that followed she came to represent something that endured far longer than her morale-boosting performances.

Through her music she inspired hope in a happier future, even when the country was on the brink of despair. But Vera also symbolised the indomitable British spirit that refused to waver or be crushed.

Her message of hope was resurrected through the song 'We'll Meet Again' during the lockdown of 2020, when people were separated from their loved ones all over the country for months on end.

Vera was born Vera Margaret Welch in 1917 in the London suburb East Ham. Her father was a plumber and her mother a dressmaker. She began performing in local clubs at an early age. By the time she was eleven she'd adopted the stage name Vera Lynn, which she borrowed from her grandmother's maiden name. Throughout the 1930s, she appeared regularly on radio and recorded dance band hits with the Joe Loss Orchestra and Charlie Kunz.

Her striking voice, along with her genuine and down-to-earth manner, endeared her to audiences. At the outbreak of war, she was ready to give up her career and join the war effort. But she was told the best contribution she could make was to carry on entertaining and boost the nation's morale.

From singing to audiences in London's Tube stations to her hugely popular radio programme *Sincerely Yours* – which broadcast messages to serving troops all over the globe – Vera lifted people's spirits across the nation, especially in the early days of the war. But she also risked her life to perform for the troops. She volunteered for the Entertainments National Service Association (ENSA), travelling thousands of miles to perform for British troops in tours throughout Egypt, India and Burma.

When the war in Europe finished in May 1940, she visited the British Fourteenth Army, who were still fighting a difficult campaign in Burma. Years later, in 1985, she was thanked for her contribution when she received the Burma Star.

In 1943, she starred in the wartime classic *We'll Meet Again*. The lyrics to the title track song epitomised British resolve and irrepressible sense of optimism. But the singer's delivery also conveyed emotions that many people across the nation were struggling to express or comprehend.

After the war, Vera's popularity refused to wane. In 1952 she became the first British artist to have a number one hit in America with the song 'Auf Wiederseh'n, Sweetheart'. Over the years, she covered many popular songs of the day and continued to perform her classic favourites at events commemorating the war.

In 2009, at the age of ninety-two, Lynn became the oldest living artist to top the British album chart. But the record breaking didn't stop there. In 2017, at the age of 100, she became the oldest singer, and first centenarian, to enter the charts with her greatest hits collection.

She also dedicated her life to many different causes and charities. She campaigned on behalf of veterans, and people who served in the Forces, and raised awareness of cerebral palsy in the 1950s, when there was very little understanding of the condition.

Vera was made OBE in 1969, a dame in 1975 and a Companion of Honour in 2016. In 2018, she received the Outstanding Contribution to Music award at the Classic Brit Awards, and, in 2000, a 'Spirit of the 20th Century' Award in a nationwide poll in which she won 21 per cent of the vote.

During lockdown, she continued to reach out to people on a personal level when she sent letters of hope and encouragement to residents in care homes. She wrote: 'Try and find the joy that remains even during these challenging times, and do what you can to help each other. As always, keep smiling through.'

In April 2020, Vera was touched that the queen referenced the lyrics 'We'll Meet Again' in a speech addressing the nation. In an interview with the *Radio Times*, she said: 'I support her message of keeping strong together when we're faced with such a terrible challenge. Our nation has faced some dark times over the years, but we always overcome.'

Vera died in June 2020. She was 103. Although she lived to an undeniably fine age, the nation was deeply saddened to hear of her death. As the country slowly began to emerge from lockdown, tributes flooded in to thank the national heroine who had made a difference to so many people's lives, even up until the end of her own.

HEROES OF
WAR

WWII

SIR NICHOLAS WINTON

Sir Nicholas Winton – often called 'the British Schindler' –
set up an organisation to rescue 669 Jewish children from
Czechoslovakia on the eve of World War II. His story
remained largely unknown, until he was reunited with
some of the children, fifty years later, on the BBC television
programme *That's Life.*

Nicholas was born in 1909, in London, to German-Jewish
parents. After he left school he worked in several banks in
France and Germany throughout the 1920s and early 30s. He
returned to London and became a broker at the London Stock
Exchange.

Throughout the 1930s, Nicholas became close friends with
several prominent members of the Labour party, including
Aneurin Bevan and Jennie Lee. They were part of a left-wing
circle that grew increasingly concerned about the threat

that Hitler and his Fascist regime posed and the British government's policy of appeasement.

As part of the Munich Agreement, Germany was promised the Sudetenland, a province in northern Czechoslovakia where three million people – mainly German-speaking – lived. Hitler stated it was his last territorial claim in Europe but he went on to invade the rest of Czechoslovakia in March 1939. Meanwhile, the Nazis' persecution of Jewish people intensified. On 9 November 1938, Hitler's paramilitary forces unleashed a wave of horrifyingly violent attacks on Jewish communities throughout Germany, Austria and the Sudetenland.

The night became known as Kristallnacht, or 'the Night of Broken Glass'. The world looked on in horror and public opinion began to turn. The British government approved a measure that would allow Jewish children under the age of seventeen into the country, provided they had a place to stay and a warranty of £50.

Towards the end of 1938, Nicholas decided to visit his friend Martin Blake, in Prague, who was helping refugees, forced to flee after the Munich Agreement.

Back in the UK, Nicholas set up an organisation to help Jewish children at risk from the Nazis, from his hotel in Wenceslas Square. For the next nine months he kept up pressure on the Home Office to give entry to eight trains with endangered children on them. With the help of his mother, he placed photographs of the children in *Picture Post* magazine and found families to accept them. It was essential he had guarantees to ensure they could obtain permission to cross into the Netherlands from Czechoslovakia.

He also wrote to politicians in other countries asking them to take more children, but only Sweden helped.

Heartbreakingly, the last train scheduled to leave Prague on 3 September 1939 was unable to depart. That day war broke out between the UK and Germany and the Czech borders were closed.

After the war Nicholas worked for the International Refugee Organisation in Paris where he met his wife Grete Gjelstrup. Her husband rarely talked about what he'd done before the war and it would be another forty years before his wife found the scrapbook that contained details of the children and the families that took them in. She handed them to a holocaust researcher and eighty of the children were found in Britain.

In 1988, Nicholas was invited on to *That's Life* as a member of the audience where his scrapbook and story was discussed. When host Esther Rantzen asked if anyone in the audience owed their life to him, more than two dozen people stood up to applaud him. When she asked if anyone present was the child or grandchild of one of the children Nicholas saved, the rest of the audience stood up and applauded. British Labour politician Alf Dubs and the immunologist Leslie Baruch Brent are just two of the notable children alive today that he saved.

Nicholas always dismissed claims he'd acted heroically, preferring to praise his colleagues Doreen Warriner and Trevor Chadwick who'd warded off attention from the Gestapo in Prague. Nevertheless, he received a slew of awards and accolades for his resolute belief that helping the children 'was the right thing to do'.

In 2003, Nicholas was knighted for services to humanity, in recognition of his work on the Czech Kindertransport. In 2010, he was named a British Hero of the Holocaust by the

British Government, and in 2014 awarded the Order of the White Lion (Class I). A statue of Nicholas stands at Prague's central station.

He died in 2015, at the age of 106.

WHEN HOST ESTHER RANTZEN ASKED IF ANYONE IN THE AUDIENCE OWED THEIR LIFE TO HIM, MORE THAN TWO DOZEN PEOPLE STOOD UP TO APPLAUD HIM. WHEN SHE ASKED IF ANYONE PRESENT WAS THE CHILD OR GRANDCHILD OF ONE OF THE CHILDREN NICHOLAS SAVED, THE REST OF THE AUDIENCE STOOD UP AND APPLAUDED.

HERBERT STANFORD

The city of Bristol was a prime target for Germany's bombing raids during World War II. As well as its shipyards – where warships were made and repaired – it was home to an airplane company that made Blenheim and Beaufort bombers for the RAF. From June 1940, the city suffered heavy bombing. But the Luftwaffe's intention to 'eliminate Bristol as an important port' was executed most intensely throughout a period of raids that began later that year. These would become known as the 'Bristol Blitz'.

One of the worst raids took place on 24 November. It began at around 6.30 in the evening. For more than six hours, 148 bombers dropped 540 tonnes of high explosives and 12,000 incendiary bombs on the city, inflicting severe damage. Within an hour over seventy fires were blazing. The number of volunteers in Bristol's Auxiliary Fire Service (AFS) had rapidly increased since the start of the war. But they were soon overwhelmed and needed reinforcements from brigades in the surrounding counties.

As fire fighters struggled to contain the flames, they faced further pressure when they had to pump water from the river, after the city's main supply was hit.

Although the Luftwaffe's main plan was to destroy the port, people who lived in the heart of the city also bore the brunt. From sounding the air-raid siren to evacuating dangerous areas, the Air Raid Wardens' Service played a vital role in protecting civilians. Herbert Stanford was just one of 800,000 people who signed up to volunteer for them.

That night, Herbert rushed to one of the worst-affected areas on Redcliff Hill. A fire had broken out after two houses had been completely destroyed by a bomb. While he evacuated residents from the adjoining houses, Herbert heard cries coming from beneath the rubble. He dropped to his knees and worked his way through the burning wreckage on his stomach, inhaling poisonous gases while the raid roared on overhead.

As he reached the group of trapped victims he saw that two of them were a young boy and girl. He gave them water and reassured them he would return with more help. However, it was harder than he first anticipated – he and his team of rescuers wouldn't be able to get them out alive by removing the debris on top. Herbert decided to make a hole in the wall that divided the building from the next house. However, they were still obstructed by debris. Undeterred, Herbert cleared a path for the team of rescuers by knocking out a fire grate. Before long, they were able to rescue the children who escaped uninjured. The raid came to an end in the early hours but Herbert continued to work through the night rescuing people that were still trapped.

As he emerged from the rubble into daylight, the city was unrecognisable. Many of its oldest buildings had been damaged or destroyed. The majority of fires were now under control but at least twenty-six continued to smoulder for another two days. In the aftermath, the Lord Mayor of Bristol, Alderman Thomas Underwood, said: 'The city of churches had in one night become the city of ruins.'

In total, 200 people were killed and a further 689 suffered injuries; 1,400 were made homeless. Yet it wasn't over for the city. A few months later, Bristol suffered another horrific raid when the city was bombed continuously for twelve hours.

In February 1941, Herbert was awarded the George Medal for bravery in Civil Defence.

HERBERT HEARD CRIES COMING FROM BENEATH THE RUBBLE. HE DROPPED TO HIS KNEES AND WORKED HIS WAY THROUGH THE BURNING WRECKAGE ON HIS STOMACH, INHALING POISONOUS GASES WHILE THE RAID ROARED ON OVERHEAD.

AS HE REACHED THE GROUP OF TRAPPED VICTIMS HE SAW THAT TWO OF THEM WERE A YOUNG BOY AND GIRL.

IDA AND LOUISE COOK

In the late 1930s, two sisters from London risked their lives to help Jewish people escape Nazi-occupied Europe. Using their adoration for opera as a cover, they regularly travelled to Germany to smuggle out valuable items that could act as financial guarantees for British immigration authorities. Ida and Louise Cook helped twenty-nine people escape. Twenty years after the war ended, they were honoured as Righteous among the Nations by the State of Israel.

Ida and Louise were both born in the early 1900s. They grew up in Sunderland originally but later moved to south London with their parents where they both took up civil service jobs. Their lives were relatively ordinary and unglamorous but for their passionate love of opera. They were ardent fans who wrote to their favourite opera stars and would wait at stage doors after they attended performances hoping to collect autographs.

In 1934, they visited the Salzburg Festival in Austria where they met and befriended the conductor and impresario Clemens Krauss and his wife, the soprano Viorica Ursuleac. It was through them that they began to learn about the Nazis' persecution of Jewish people living in Germany. At this stage, Jews were able to leave the country but weren't allowed to take money or possessions with them. It was only possible for them to start a new life in Great Britain if they had a job to go to or sufficient funds to live on.

The sisters found a way to help. As well as a passion for opera, Ida was a prolific and successful writer who had a skill for writing romantic fiction. In 1936, she published her first novel as Mary Burchell. As Ida's books began to sell, the women were able to fund more frequent trips abroad.

On Friday night they flew from Croydon Airport to the opera houses of Germany and Austria. On the Sunday they returned by train in time for Louise to get to work on Monday. Only the two women weren't only attending shows at the opera any more. On each trip the sisters would arrive plain-clothed before they departed, draped in jewellery and furs that were passed off as their own. Ida and Louise always ensured they used different checkpoints on arrival and departure so that they didn't meet the same officials twice and arouse suspicion.

It was a risky operation. The sisters were knowingly smuggling goods out of the country, which was against the law. They also faced the continual threat of inspection from SS guards, who were tightening their control at the borders as war between the UK and Germany looked increasingly likely. On many occasions their bags were stuffed to the brim with valuables. If they'd been caught they would have been imprisoned and the British government wouldn't have been able to help them. The sisters invented various cover stories in case their bags were ever searched – one included pretending they always travelled with their jewellery because they didn't trust their relatives back home.

As well as smuggling out valuables, the sisters also persuaded people to offer work to the refugees or put down financial deposits that would satisfy the Home Office. They bought a flat at Dolphin Square in Pimlico, south-west London where the refugees could stay comfortably until they were settled. Where possible, the sisters tried to keep families together and Louise taught herself German so that she could communicate better with them. On one occasion Ida nearly broke down in tears at the thought of all the people they wouldn't be able to save.

After the war Ida wrote her memoir *We Followed the Stars*. It touched briefly on the people they'd helped before the war but it focused mainly on their love for opera. Neither of the sisters would talk about their experiences unless they were asked.

In 1965, the sisters received the Righteous Among the Nations honour from the Yad Vashem Martyrs and Heroes Remembrance authority in the State of Israel – given to non-Jews who took great risks to save Jewish people during the Holocaust. They were praised for their 'warmth of heart, devotion, rare perseverance [and willingness] to sacrifice their personal safety, time and energy'.

Ida died in 1986. Louise died in 1991. In 2010 they were posthumously awarded as Heroes of the Holocaust by the British government.

> **ON MANY OCCASIONS THEIR BAGS WERE STUFFED TO THE BRIM WITH VALUABLES. IF THEY'D BEEN CAUGHT THEY WOULD HAVE BEEN IMPRISONED AND THE BRITISH GOVERNMENT WOULDN'T HAVE BEEN ABLE TO HELP THEM.**

FLYING OFFICER GORDON CLEAVER

By the summer of 1940, RAF Tangmere in West Sussex, along with many other airfields along the south coast, was as prepared as it could be for a large-scale assault from the Luftwaffe. The surrounding villages had been evacuated and its airfield had been enlarged to make way for faster fighter aircraft – as well as Spitfires, these included Hawker Furies and Hurricanes, which would play a pivotal role in the Battle of Britain.

On 16 August, Tangmere suffered a ferocious attack from a large force of German dive-bombers that inflicted severe damage on the airfield. All the hangars were destroyed and the power, water and sanitation systems were put out of action. However, despite being significantly outnumbered, the Tangmere squadrons did not give up without a fight. Hurricanes and Spitfires destroyed nine enemy dive-bombers and badly damaged seven more.

Flying Officer Gordon Cleaver was just one of the pilots on duty that day defending the base in his Hurricane. He was already widely celebrated for courageous and successful attempts at destroying enemy aircraft during earlier operations in France and the Dunkirk evacuation. In this particular raid he showed equal bravery and determination when he took on, and destroyed, one of the German aircraft.

However, during the attack, Gordon's sight was severely impaired when a shell shattered the cockpit's hood and sent Perspex splinters flying into his eyes. His aircraft was also significantly damaged. He was in desperate pain but refused to abandon his aircraft and managed to land the hurricane successfully. Gordon was rushed to hospital where the doctors managed to save his sight partially. Although his career as a pilot was over, he remained in the RAF until 1943.

In September 1940, Gordon was awarded the Distinguished Flying Cross for his bravery during the raid on Tangmere, despite suffering horrific injuries. Forty years later, his sight was restored after an operation.

VIOLETTE SZABO

Violette Szabo defied convention from the start. As a young girl she learnt to shoot and quickly earned a reputation for being a crack shot among the male members of her family. She also stood out at school in south London, attracting admirers for her fluency in French due to her bilingual upbringing. She was probably always destined for a life less ordinary.

But at the outbreak of World War II it's unlikely anyone could have foreseen, including Violette, just what an extraordinary legacy she'd leave. Over seventy years later, she is still regarded as one of the bravest women in British history, with a story that defies belief as well as conventionality.

In 1940, at the age of nineteen, Violette met and married Etienne Szabo, an officer in the French Foreign Legion. After their marriage she took a job as a switchboard operator for the Post Office in London. But she soon left because she was bored. In September 1941, she enlisted in the Auxiliary Territorial Service (ATS) where she trained to work in one of the first mixed anti-aircraft batteries in Oswestry, Shropshire.

However, Violette found out she was pregnant and left to return to London. In June 1942, she gave birth to her daughter Tania. Later that year Etienne died in action during the Second Battle of El Alamein. It was around this time that Violette attracted the attention of the British Special Operations Executive (SOE), due to her fluency in French and training in the ATS. She accepted their offer to train as a field agent, determined to fight the enemy that killed her husband.

Throughout 1943, Violette trained in fieldcraft, navigation, weapons and demolition. She also received training in escape, communications and cryptography. In the final stages of training she was taught to parachute jump but sprained her ankle and was sent home for recuperation. A popular member of the SOE, she was known for her impetuous nature, infectious sense of fun and Cockney accent.

In February 1944, Violette passed the parachuting course she needed for her first mission into France. During this time she met Philippe Liewer, the organiser of Salesman, one of the SOE's resistance circuits. In April 1944, they were dropped into German-occupied France. Under the codename Louise, Violette travelled throughout Rouen and Dieppe to gather intelligence on local factories producing war materials for the Germans. In the process she also discovered that Philippe's network had been broken up. Despite being arrested, the mission was successful and she returned to England at the end of the month.

On the evening of 7 June, immediately after D-Day, Violette and Philippe were sent on another mission to France. They were headed for the outskirts of Limoges, a city in west central France, to coordinate local resistance networks and re-establish a network of saboteurs, as the Germans attempted to stem the Allied advance through Normandy. However, Violette was re-directed by Philippe to the Dordogne to coordinate resistance activity with another network.

On the morning of the 10th, Violette set off on her mission in a car driven by a young resistance fighter called Jacques Dufour. This was against Philippe's better judgement, who'd wanted her to go by bicycle as the Germans had forbidden the use of cars after D-Day.

Violette was armed with a Sten gun and eight magazines of ammunition. Their car raised the suspicions of German troops at a roadblock that had been set up to find a battalion commander who'd been captured by the local resistance. Violette and Jacques leapt from the car and a gun battle ensued. As armoured cars arrived on the scene they attempted to escape through a field. However, as they ran up a hill to find cover from some trees Violette fell and twisted her ankle. She refused Jacques' offer of help and urged him to flee. She then struggled to a nearby tree where she fought off the Germans in pursuit for thirty minutes, giving Jacques enough time to make his escape. During the gun battle, she killed a corporal and wounded some other soldiers.

Eventually, Violette ran out of ammunition and was captured by two SS troops who dragged her up the hill to a bridge. Here, she was questioned by a young officer who was so impressed by her heroic performance that he congratulated her.

After she was interrogated for four days by SS troops in Limoges she was transferred to Fresnes Prison in Paris and brought to Gestapo headquarters, who now knew her true identity as an SOE agent. Violette was then sent to Germany, shackled to Denise Bloch, another SOE wireless operator. After a gruelling eighteen-day journey they arrived in the notorious women-only concentration camp, Ravensbrück.

For the next five months she endured malnutrition, hard labour in freezing cold temperatures and horrific conditions. But Violette's courageous spirit refused to break. She helped save the life of a young Belgian resistance fighter, kept the morale of other women in the camp, and constantly planned to escape. In October 1944, she was sent to a factory along with 1000 French women, which included Denise Bloch and the French resistance fighter Lilian Rolfe. They were ordered to make munitions but refused. Later that month she was sent back to Ravensbrück then transferred to a punishment camp at Königsberg in Poland where she was forced to fell trees in bitterly cold winds, dressed only in summer clothes. At night she slept in freezing cold barracks without blankets.

Even in these unimaginable conditions, Violette remained hopeful and optimistic. However, in January 1945 she was sent back to Ravensbrück and placed in a punishment bunker where she was held in solitary confinement and most likely beaten.

The following month, Violette was executed. She was just twenty-three. Denise Bloch and Lilian Rolfe were also killed.

In 1946 Violette was awarded the George Cross posthumously for her extraordinary bravery. Her daughter Tania collected the award. In 1947 the French government awarded her the Croix de Guerre and she is listed on the Valençay SOE memorial as one of the agents who died liberating France. Violette and Etienne are the most decorated married couple of World War II.

EVENTUALLY, VIOLETTE RAN OUT OF AMMUNITION AND WAS CAPTURED BY TWO SS TROOPS WHO DRAGGED HER UP THE HILL TO A BRIDGE. HERE, SHE WAS QUESTIONED BY A YOUNG OFFICER WHO WAS SO IMPRESSED BY HER HEROIC PERFORMANCE THAT HE CONGRATULATED HER.

ODETTE HALLOWES

Odette Hallowes was the first of three women to be awarded the George Cross in World War II. She was also the only one who survived the war and lived to tell the world about her experiences.

Odette was born Odette Marie Léonie Céline Brailly, in Amiens, France in 1912. Her father was killed at Verdun shortly before the Armistice and was posthumously awarded the Croix de Guerre for heroism. As a child she contracted polio, which left her bedridden for months, and other serious illnesses, one of which blinded her for three and a half years. In 1931 she married an Englishman Roy Sansom and moved to Britain. They had three children. At the outbreak of war, Roy joined the army, while she moved the children to safety in Somerset.

In the spring of 1942, Odette came to the attention of the Special Operations Executive (SOE) by chance. The Admiralty appealed for photographs taken on the French coastline that could prove useful for the war effort. She gathered some together and accidentally sent them to the War Office. As a result, and with her knowledge of the French language, she was invited to join the 'F' section, which sent agents into France to work with the resistance against the German occupying forces. Odette was torn between leaving her children and wanting to help. In the end, it was the harrowing stories she heard from her family in France that convinced her to go.

As cover for her secret work Odette was enrolled in the First Aid Nursing Yeomanry (FANY) which supplied SOE with support personnel. Odette was trained in self-defence, Morse code and how to resist interrogation. She was described as 'excitable and temperamental' by the SOE but extremely patriotic to France.

On 31 October 1942, Odette arrived in Cannes under her codename 'Lise'. She was met by Peter Churchill and joined his resistance network, Spindle. Her initial mission was to contact the resistance on the French Riviera and establish a safe house for agents in Burgundy. Odette had doubts surrounding the loyalty of some members of the network and she, along with Peter and another agent, Adolphe Rabinovitch, moved to the Italian-occupied Annecy area in the French Alps.

However, they were caught by the spy-catcher Hugo Bleicher, who'd discovered their location from a double agent. Odette and Peter were arrested. Odette was sent to Fresnes Prison near Paris. She sought to protect Peter and stuck to a fabricated story they'd previously created, which they hoped could help them in future bargaining – that Peter was Winston Churchill's nephew, she was married to him, and he was only in the country on her insistence.

Odette was brutally tortured fourteen times by the Gestapo for information on her fellow agents. But she refused to tell them anything. To every question, she replied: 'I have nothing to say.' In later years, Odette said that the pain she suffered as a child helped her endure the ordeal. She also focused on getting through each minute, rather than imagining what could happen in the next half hour. Odette's refusal to reveal any names saved the lives of many resistance fighters.

In July 1944, Odette was sent to Ravensbrück concentration camp. She was held in solitary confinement for over three months without light and placed on a starvation diet. She was sentenced to death on several occasions but her captors' belief that she was related to Winston Churchill stopped them from carrying out the execution.

On 3 May 1945, she was escorted to Allied lines by the camp commandant Fritz Suhren. He'd hoped her connections to Churchill might help him in future negotiations, but he was arrested by the Americans. Odette later testified against him at the Hamburg Ravensbrück trials and he was executed in 1950.

Odette went on to become World War II's most-decorated spy. In 1946, she was awarded an MBE and the George Cross for refusing to reveal the name of her fellow agents. She accepted her medal on behalf of all her comrades who did not survive. She was also awarded the Chevalier de la Légion d'honneur for her work with the French Resistance and five other medals.

Odette divorced her first husband Roy and went on to marry Peter Churchill in 1947. Ten years later she divorced Peter and married Geoffrey Hallowes. In 1949, she published her biography and her story was made into a film in 1950.

Odette became a celebrated heroine on both sides of the Channel. She died in 1995 at the age of eighty-two.

ODETTE WENT ON TO BECOME WORLD WAR II'S MOST DECORATED SPY. IN 1946, SHE WAS AWARDED AN MBE AND THE GEORGE CROSS FOR REFUSING TO REVEAL THE NAME OF HER FELLOW AGENTS. SHE ACCEPTED HER MEDAL ON BEHALF OF ALL HER COMRADES WHO DID NOT SURVIVE.

OPERATION CROSSBOW

Throughout the last few years of World War II, the RAF Bomber Command carried out a set of audacious raids that struck at Germany's infamous V-weapon launch sites. These operations helped significantly limit attacks from flying bombs and rockets that were wreaking havoc on British cities. However, the raids wouldn't have been possible without the help of the unarmed reconnaissance pilots, who risked their lives flying in enemy territory to take aerial photographs.

In 1940, the RAF created the Photograph Reconnaissance Unit. Their secret weapon wasn't a bomb or a rocket: it was a Victorian invention called a stereoscope that generated three-dimensional images of enemy landscape. These were analysed by a team of photographic interpreters (PIs) at RAF Medmenham in Buckinghamshire. On closer inspection, they were able to identify structures that included rockets and launch sites.

Jimmy Taylor was just one of the reconnaissance pilots who undertook these extremely difficult and dangerous missions. For the 3D effect to work, the photos had to be captured in a series of specific sequences, which took a huge amount of skill on the part of the pilot. They were among the best in the air force, although many lost their lives because the operations were so risky. They flew unarmed at 30,000 feet – due to the weight of five cameras – and were therefore completely at the mercy of enemy fire.

The reconnaissance pilots gathered many images that would prove vital to the Allied war effort. But it was Operation Crossbar that altered the course of the war and reduced the number of civilian casualties. In 1942, a spitfire flying over

Peenemünde in north-eastern Germany spotted an airfield with three concrete-and-earth circles. Reconnaissance pilots were sent to investigate – some of the bravest flew as low as thirty metres to ensure they got the clearest images.

PIs worked throughout the night to analyse the pictures and confirmed that the area was a research centre developing V-missiles. In the summer of 1944, the V-1 – known as the doodlebug – brought terror to the capital. On 17 and 18 August, 500 bombers were sent to destroy Peenemünde, disrupting the V-2 programme and killing senior Nazi scientists. Unfortunately, the Germans began using less conspicuous launch sites and mobile missiles. In September, the deathly silent V-2 crashed in Chiswick and demolished eleven houses. However, the bombers, using intelligence gathered by reconnaissance pilots, were still able to attack supporting infrastructure around the launch sites.

Originally, the Germans had planned to launch up to 2000 rockets a day, but the work of everyone involved in Operation Crossbar severely hampered their original mission. Germany was also unable to launch a wave of devastating attacks on the UK, which could have threatened the D-Day landings and significantly prolonged the war.

THE DAM BUSTERS

Operation Chastise became known as one of the most memorable of RAF Bomber Command's raids because it achieved what was previously thought impossible. In 1943, nineteen Lancaster heavy bombers – immortalised in the 1955 British film *The Dam Busters*

– struck at Nazi Germany's industrial heartland with one of the most innovative inventions of the twentieth century. Barnes Wallis's 'bouncing bomb' breached two dams in the Ruhr valley, destroying twelve war production factories in the process and damaging 100 more. The raid significantly hampered German war production and forced them to reallocate resources away from their defensive effort.

Before World War II broke out, the British Air Ministry had already identified the dams as important strategic targets. They provided power and water for steel making and supplied water for the canal transport system. The ministry knew that destroying the dam would wreak havoc on hundreds of factories and, if successful, could significantly tip the outcome of the war in the Allies favour. But the RAF lacked a weapon strong enough for the job. They turned to aviation engineer Barnes Wallis for solutions. At first, he wanted to drop a ten-tonne bomb from 40,000 feet, but no aircraft was able to fly at that altitude or carry such a heavy weapon. The dams were also protected by heavy torpedo nets to prevent warheads from reaching the dams' walls under the water.

Eventually, Barnes designed a bomb in the shape of a cylinder. It was lighter in weight, and engineered to achieve a backward spin of 500 rotations per minute. If the bomb was dropped from 60 feet at 240 miles an hour, it could skip across the surface of the water, before hitting the dam wall and submerging under water towards the base. There were many technical problems to solve and the operation depended on the ability of the squadron's most-skilled pilots – for the raid to succeed they had to fly at night over enemy territory at altitudes of 100 feet or less.

At 9.28pm on 16 May, 133 men took off from RAF Scampton in nineteen bombers aimed at three separate targets. Many didn't make it – one flew so low that it hit the sea, while another flew into electricity cables. Eight bombers were shot down. But the squadron did succeed. Wing Commander Guy Gibson descended to just a few feet above the water of the Moehne dam to make the initial attack and took the full brunt of the anti-aircraft defences. He then circled low for a further thirty minutes to draw in enemy fire on himself, in turn enabling the following aircraft to attack the dam. He then flew the squadron on to the Eder dam where they repeated these tactics – both dams were destroyed while a third, the Sorpe, was also significantly damaged.

Two power stations were destroyed and seven others were damaged. Germany lost 400,000 tonnes' worth of coal production in the month of May. Thousands of forced labourers were transferred from the coast of Normandy and other sites to repair the damages.

Of the nineteen bombers, eleven returned the following morning. Fifty-three Allied personnel were killed and another three captured. Thirty-four of the survivors were decorated at Buckingham Palace and Wing Commander Guy Gibson was awarded the Victoria Cross for leading the breach of the Moehne and Eder dams. For the seventy-fifth anniversary of the raid, artist Dan Llywelyn Hall painted portraits of all 133 men who took part in the raid.

There is a memorial to the fallen members of the squadron at RAF Woodhall Spa airbase, the last home of the squadron during World War II.

NOOR INAYAT KHAN

In 2018, interest in Noor Inayat Khan's extraordinary story was revived when the World War II spy was proposed as the new face of the £50 note, the first from an ethnic minority.

Noor was raised to be a pacifist by her Sufi preacher father, but she abhorred Nazi tyranny and vowed to fight it. She was recruited as a secret agent by the elite Special Operations Executive (SEO) and became the first woman wireless operator to be sent into France. Noor is one of only four women to be awarded the George Cross – the highest civilian decoration in the UK – for her extraordinary courage during World War II.

Noor was born in 1914 in Moscow. Her father came from a noble Indian Muslim family. He taught Sufism and met his American wife when she attended one of his lectures in San Francisco. Noor's family left Russia for London when she was a baby before the outbreak of World War I. She attended nursery at Notting Hill before they moved to Paris in 1920.

Her parents raised her to be tolerant of all religions. A creative and sensitive girl, she studied Psychology at the Sorbonne and music at the Paris Conservatory. She composed for harp and piano and wrote poetry and children's stories. In 1939, her book *Twenty Jataka Tales* – inspired by tales from the Buddhist tradition – was published.

In June 1940, Noor and her family fled to Cornwall, England when France was overrun by German troops. She couldn't bear to see any country occupied and in November of that year she joined the WAAF, determined to help defeat the Nazis. She trained to be a wireless operator and was soon recruited by the SOE for her fluency in French and signalling skills.

In February 1943, she was seconded to First Aid Nursing Yeomanry (FANY) and received special training as a wireless operator in occupied territory. Her skill as a harpist proved invaluable – she was a fast and accurate signaller. She was a pacifist at heart and struggled to handle weapons at first. However, she worked hard to overcome this.

In June 1943, she was sent to France where she posed as a children's nurse. Madeleine was her codename. Her role as a wireless operator was extremely difficult and dangerous – it was relatively simple for the enemy to intercept operators' messages if they stayed on the air transmitting for longer than twenty minutes. Each time the operator moved location they had to carry the bulky transmitter with them, normally concealed in a suitcase. In 1943, the average life expectancy of an operator was six weeks.

Within ten days of Noor's arrival, all the other British

agents in her network had been arrested. The SOE urged her to return but she decided to stay and try to rebuild the network. For the next three months, she ran a cell single-handedly. She was on the move constantly and changed her appearance regularly to evade detection as she carried the wireless set around. Her work was crucial to the war effort – she was the only link between agents in Paris and London, taking on the work of at least six operators.

But Noor was eventually betrayed, possibly by Henri Déricourt, who was a double agent. In October 1943, she was captured by the Gestapo, just as she was about to leave for England.

She tried to escape but was caught and sent to a German prison in Pforzheim, on the edge of the Black Forest. For the next ten months, she was chained in solitary confinement, starved, beaten and tortured. Despite this, she never revealed any information. Noor was classified as 'highly dangerous' and shackled in chains most of the time.

On 12 September 1944, she was sent to the Dachau concentration camp. She and three other fellow agents – Yolande Beekman, Madeleine Damerment and Éliane Plewman were executed the next day. Her last word was simply 'Liberté'. She was thirty.

Noor was posthumously awarded the George Cross in 1949, and a French Croix de Guerre. She was the third of three women to be awarded the George Cross in World War II. In 2012 a sculpture of the agent was unveiled close to her former London home in Gordon Square Gardens. Noor is also commemorated at the Air Forces Memorial, one of the 20,000 airmen and women who were lost in World War II and have no known grave.

In 2011, the Noor Inayat Khan Memorial Trust was established to promote the principles Noor stood for – peace, non-violence, and religious and racial harmony. The trust works with schools, universities and museums to ensure her incredible story and heroism is never forgotten.

IN 1943, THE AVERAGE LIFE EXPECTANCY OF AN OPERATOR WAS SIX WEEKS.

THOMAS KIRBY-GREEN

Thomas Kirby-Green was well known for his lively and gregarious nature – as well as his unusually decorated bunk at the Stalag Luft III in Poland. But it's his courageous actions on the night of 24 March 1944 that have assured his legacy as one of the real-life heroes of the notorious prisoner of war camp, immortalised years later in the film *The Great Escape*.

Thomas was born in 1918 and grew up in the town of Dowa in modern-day Malawi, where his father was British District Governor. He was sent to boarding school in the UK. When he left, he went to live with his parents in Tangier before joining the RAF in Egypt in May 1937. A month later he was confirmed as a pilot officer.

Not long after the outbreak of war, he joined No. 9 Squadron RAF to fly Vicker Wellingtons. By the end of 1940 he'd completed twenty-seven operations. That September he was posted to a newly formed Czech squadron as flight instructor. A highly skilled pilot, he took part in a bombing attack on Turin, Italy and was the only pilot in his squadron who successfully bombed the target.

A month later he took off from RAF Alconbury to bomb factories in Duisburg but was shot down near Reichswald Forest in north Germany. He was the only one of his crew to survive, but was captured and taken to Stalag Luft camp in Sagen, eastern Germany. As a prisoner of war, he was able to write letters home to his wife Maria and receive presents from his family. Despite the tough conditions in the camp, he remained a bright and effusive character, known for his gramophone records of Latin music and bright clothing that his family sent from Tangiers. He also taught Spanish to the other prisoners.

A few months later he was transferred to Stalag Luft III. It was here he got to know Roger Bushell and Roy Langlois who were plotting an escape out of the camp, even though the Germans believed it was completely escape proof – the sandy soil in the camp's surrounding area meant that tunnelling out was difficult. Tom was recruited as senior security officer for the escape committee. He became known as Big S, overseeing a watchout on German activities and collating information on Spain to assist escapers heading there.

The three began to dig three tunnels, thirty feet below the surface, along with other RAF officers, codenamed Tom, Dick and Harry. The sandy walls were supported with wood they scavenged. They hid the dug-out soil in their trousers before scattering it around the camp.

Just before the escape attempt, Tom, as he was known, wrote what he knew could be his last letter to his wife: 'My beloved and adored darling, I am thinking so much of you and long for you with every part of my soul and body.'

Tom was paired with Gordon Kidder. Halfway through the escape out of the tunnel, he was almost buried when part of it caved in. However, they were among the first twenty-four of seventy-six men who managed to escape the prison camp just before the alarm was sounded. When they aroused suspicion at the local train station they were questioned by a policeman. But they managed to convince him they were Spanish labourers.

They boarded the train for Breslau where they changed trains for Czechoslovakia, hoping for a connection to Yugoslavia or Hungary where Thomas had friends. But after they crossed the border they were recaptured and briefly held at Zlin prison. They were then driven to the Czech town of Hrabuvka where members of the Gestapo executed them, along with forty-eight other recaptured prisoners. Thomas was just twenty-six.

Only three of the escapees managed to make it back home. A total of seventy-three were recaptured and fifty were executed on the orders of Hitler. After the war, a number of those guilty of the murders were tracked down, arrested and tried for their crimes.

In 2011, Thomas's son Colin made a pilgrimage to the spot where his father died. He discovered that locals had commemorated his father and Gordon Kidder with a memorial.

TUBBY CLAYTON

Philip 'Tubby' Clayton served as a priest during World War I in France and Flanders, where he opened a refuge, Talbot House, for soldiers on leave. The spirit of friendship he fostered there sparked the international 'Toc H' movement, which continues to support communities all over the world today.

In 1922, Tubby became vicar of All Hallows by the Tower in London, which brought him into contact with impoverished parts of the East End. He helped set up the Tower Hill Improvement Trust, which demolished old and derelict buildings to make way for gardens and open spaces for the public. The Trust also brought in 1,500 barge-loads of sand to create a beach on the banks of the river at Tower Hill. In 1934, it was opened to the public and King George V announced that the children of London should have 'free access for ever'. The beach was a huge success for many East End families who couldn't afford trips to the seaside.

Throughout World War II, Tubby witnessed the devastation that the Blitz brought to All Hallows and the East End. He began fundraising for their restoration. In 1948, he joined forces with John G Winant, the US Ambassador to the UK, and set up the Winant Clayton Volunteer Association. The charity brought young Americans to London to help with the restoration and rebuilding of Tower Hamlets and the East End. In 1959, the charity helped send British people to New York to volunteer on similar projects that supported disadvantaged groups. It was the start of an annual exchange programme that aimed to promote friendship and cultural understanding through volunteering. The scheme continued for many decades after the war.

Tubby died in 1972. He is honoured in The Museum of Army Chaplaincy near Swindon and Talbot House museum in Poperinge, Belgium.

GILLIAN 'BOBBIE' TANNER

Gillian Wilton-Clark (then Gillian 'Bobbie' Tanner) was one of 70,000 women who had enrolled in the National Fire Service (NFS) by 1943. Although they were trained they didn't fight fires in World War II. But many were recognised for their bravery, especially during the Blitz in 1940, when London was bombed for fifty-seven nights in a row.

When war broke out on 3 September 1939, nineteen-year-old Gillian drove to London from her home near Cirencester, in Gloucestershire to see what she could do to help. She approached The Women's Voluntary Service (WVS) who directed her to the NFS. Gillian was posted to Dock Head. She was one of only two drivers who had a heavy goods licence, so she was tasked with driving the canteen van and petrol lorry. At the time, health and safety was practically non-existent – the petrol was stacked in two-gallon tins on shelves around the lorry. Gillian was often required to deliver cups of tea and sandwiches to firemen on shifts.

But on 20 September 1940, at the height of the Blitz, she risked her life to deliver a lorry full of petrol to firemen at Bermondsey docks. While the city blazed, Gillian drove through the streets of London in blackout, avoiding craters and rubble to ensure they could refuel the fire pumps at the docks.

Gillian was the only female fire fighter to be awarded the George Medal during World War II for her bravery that night. She even had a fire station named in her honour.

Gillian got married in 1945. She stayed with the service until she became pregnant. But she continued to drive after the war and took a job driving goods in a ten-tonne lorry. In the 1950s she competed in the Monte Carlo rally four times, finishing second once, and later turned down a contract to drive for Mini.

In 2005, Gillian attended the unveiling of a million-pound bronze sculpture to commemorate the role of women during World War Two. She was among seven surviving medal-holders at the Whitehall service. She died in 2016, at the age of ninety-six.

BETTY POPKISS

At the outbreak of World War II, Betty Popkiss joined St John Ambulance in Coventry as a volunteer. It was her first job after leaving school. Throughout October and November 1940, Coventry suffered particularly heavy air raids, with 400 bombers destroying large sections of the city, including the cathedral.

On the evening of 19 October 1940, Betty called into the Air-Raid Precautions post near her home in Hen Lane, Holbrooks. That night, not long after the signal was sounded, slow-burning incendiaries began to fall. It was a race against time to put them out before they caught fire. Despite being terrified of heights, Betty climbed up into the loft of one house to help a man who was trying to stop his home from catching fire.

As Betty headed home, the bombers began to drop heavy explosives. A girl came running towards her crying for help. Betty directed her to the ARP post to get more help. As Betty rushed down the street she realised that there had been a direct hit on the Anderson shelter that belonged to the family who lived next door to her. Betty began to dig in the rubble with her bare hands until she found a spade nearby to use. She could hear people calling out in distress underneath the debris. She had no light to help her in the rescue operation, other than the shells exploding overhead, but she kept digging to free the family. In total there were seven people trapped within the rubble. Betty laid her coat over them to keep them warm and provided basic first aid.

Betty was just seventeen when she was awarded the George Medal for her bravery. Two years later she left the UK for South Africa with her husband. She returned for the first time in sixty years in 2005 to attend the unveiling of the memorial in Whitehall, which honours the role of women in World War II.

ALAN TURING

Alan Turing is widely considered to be the founding father of computer science and artificial intelligence. His pioneering work at Bletchley Park, the top-secret home of the World War II code breakers, is estimated to have shortened the war by at least two years and saved the lives of over fourteen million people. Despite these incredible achievements he never received the full acclaim or attention he deserved in his lifetime, due to his homosexuality and the fact most of his work was covered under the Official Secrets Act. He died a social pariah at the age of forty-two.

Alan was born in London in 1912. From an early age he displayed flashes of genius and at school his teachers recognised his precocious talent. In 1926 Alan went to Sherborne School at the age of thirteen, where he showed incredible ability in maths and science, and was able to solve advanced problems in calculus without having studied it. While there he formed a close friendship with a fellow pupil, Christopher Collan Morcom, who shared his passion for maths and science and introduced Alan to astronomy. He was heartbroken when Christopher died at eighteen from tuberculosis. Alan never forgot him and the close friendship they shared would inspire his work years later.

After Sherborne he studied at King's College in Cambridge where he graduated with a first in maths. In 1936, his paper on computable numbers was published in the *London Mathematical Society* journal. It proved that a universal computing machine – which would become known as the Turing machine – could perform any mathematic computation if presented as an algorithm.

In the late 1930s, Alan studied at Princeton University, New Jersey and obtained a PhD from the department of mathematics, where he introduced the concept of ordinal logic and relative computing. He returned to the UK and began working with British codebreaking organisation the Government Code and Cypher School (GC&CS).

When war broke out in 1939, Alan took up a full-time role at Bletchley Park, in Buckinghamshire, the wartime station of GC&CS. He set to work deciphering military codes sent by Germany's Enigma machine. Although Polish cryptologists had already designed a machine to break the code, the Germans updated their security at the outbreak of war and changed the cypher system daily.

Alan developed a new codebreaking machine based on their original design, called the Bombe. It was designed to perform a chain of logical deductions that were based on a fragment of probable plain text. From mid-1940 the machine was helping codebreakers gather significant amounts of intelligence that contributed to the war effort.

By the summer of 1941, shipping losses had fallen to under 10,000 tons a month, but they desperately needed more staff and Bombe machines to keep on top of the Germans. In October they wrote directly to Winston Churchill who immediately supplied them with more resources. By the end of the war more than 200 Bombes were in operation. Alan's role was essential in helping the Allies in 1942 during the Battle of the Atlantic.

After the war, Alan continued his research on the universal computing machine – which came to be known as the Turing machine – incorporating what he'd learnt during the war. During this time he published a design for the ACE (Automatic Computing Engine), which helped lay the foundations for the modern computer.

In 1946, Turing was appointed an Officer of the Order of the British Empire (OBE) by King George VI for his wartime services. But his role in cracking the Enigma code was kept secret until the 1970s and the full extent of his contribution wasn't known until the 90s.

In 1952, Alan was found guilty of gross indecency. He avoided a prison sentence by accepting chemical castration.

Two years later, he was found dead. An inquest ruled that it was suicide. His impact on computer science is now widely acknowledged. Since 1966, the annual Turing Award recognises the 'highest distinction in computer science' and is considered to be the 'Nobel Prize of Computing'.

In 2013 the queen signed a pardon for Turing's conviction for 'gross indecency'. The Alan Turing law is now an informal term that pardons men who were convicted under legislation that outlawed homosexual acts. In 2019, the Bank of England announced that Alan had been chosen to appear on the new fifty-pound note.

BY THE END OF THE WAR MORE THAN 200 BOMBERS WERE IN OPERATION. ALAN'S ROLE WAS ESSENTIAL IN HELPING THE ALLIES IN 1942 DURING THE BATTLE OF THE ATLANTIC.

DUNKIRK NURSES

On 10 May 1940, Germany invaded France and the Low Countries. As a result, hundreds of thousands of Belgian, British and French troops were pushed back to the French port Dunkirk, where they were cut off and surrounded by German troops on the beaches of the French port Dunkirk.

The Royal Navy launched an enormous rescue mission that lasted eight days.

Over 800 naval vessels, and hundreds of small civilian boats, transported troops across the English Channel. The RAF also assisted in the mission, intercepting German bombers above the beach.

However, little is known about the brave nurses who also risked their lives during Operation Dynamo. At the start of World War II, nurses from the Queen Alexandra's Imperial Military Nursing Service (QAIMNS), were sent to France with the British Army to set up hospitals.

When the evacuation of Dunkirk was ordered, they helped destroy the buildings and any equipment that could be of use to the enemy. But they also helped to bring back thousands of servicemen, many of them wounded, to the safety of England.

Although the nurses travelled in hospital ships that were clearly marked with a large white and red cross, they were still targeted by the Luftwaffe. They were left to the mercy of German aircraft, with no means to defend themselves. Their survival depended solely on whether RAF aircraft could come to their aid in time. However, even under these difficult conditions many of the nurses managed to remain calm and carry on tending to the wounded.

There were also several nurses who worked on the hospital trains in the field hospitals. Lillian Gutteridge was one of the last nurses to make her way to Dunkirk to await evacuation. As she drove an ambulance of wounded men to safety, she was stopped by an SS officer who tried to take control of the vehicle and ordered his men to throw out the stretcher-bound patients. She refused to hand them over and slapped the officer's face. He responded by stabbing her in the thigh but was shot down by passing Black Watch soldiers.

Despite her injury, Lillian continued to drive the ambulance. She drove the wounded patients to a railway and persuaded a French train driver to take them on board. During the journey they collected another 600 wounded French and British personnel. Several days later they arrived safely in England. Many of the nurses received Royal Red Cross medals for their part in the evacuations.

Churchill and his advisers had predicted it would only be possible to rescue around 30,000 men. But over 338,000 British, French and Belgian troops were rescued from the beaches of Dunkirk.

ALTHOUGH THE NURSES TRAVELLED IN HOSPITAL SHIPS THAT WERE CLEARLY MARKED WITH A LARGE WHITE AND RED CROSS, THEY WERE STILL TARGETED BY THE LUFTWAFFE. THEY WERE LEFT TO THE MERCY OF GERMAN AIRCRAFT, WITH NO MEANS TO DEFEND THEMSELVES.

AMAZING
ANIMALS

WWII

Judy was a pedigree pointer who won the hearts of the
nation for her heroics during World War II. She is still the
only animal to be officially recognised as a Prisoner of War
(POW).

In 1942, Judy was on board the HMS *Grasshopper*, south
of Singapore. After an attack from Japanese aircraft left the
crew shipwrecked on a desert island, she led survivors to the
only source of fresh water. However, they were eventually
captured and Judy, along with the surviving British sailors,
was sent to the infamous Death Railway in Burma. While
she was imprisoned, she became known for her courage
in defending POWs from the brutality of the camp guards.
According to various sources, Judy would fly to the side of
the man taking a beating and begin to growl and snarl at the
aggressors – as the attackers were momentarily distracted,
Judy bore the brunt of the butts of their rifles. Incredibly,
though, she survived the war and was eventually adopted by
former fellow prisoner Frank Williams.

Judy was awarded the PDSA Dickin Medal (the equivalent of the Victoria Cross) for 'magnificent courage and endurance in Japanese prison camps, which helped maintain morale among fellow prisoners and also saved many lives through intelligence and watchfulness'. In 2015, her story was published in *Judy: A Dog in a Million*.

At least eight other dogs were awarded for their heroism during World War II. These include two Alsatians known as Irma and Khan.

Irma helped rescue 191 victims during the Blitz, when she served with London's Civil Defence Services. She was particularly well known for her ability to tell if buried victims were dead or alive. In 1945, she was awarded the Dickin Medal for 'bravery in locating victims trapped under blitzed buildings'. She is buried in the PDSA Animal Cemetery in Ilford.

In November 1944, Khan was sent to the island of Walcheren in the Netherlands with the sixth battalion of the Cameronians (Scottish Rifles). Corporal James Muldoon was his handler. The island was of strategic importance and needed to be taken so that the invasion of Germany could take place.

As Khan and Muldoon approached the island by sea, their boat came under heavy fire. It capsized, sending the crew into the water. Khan swam to shore but Muldoon couldn't swim and was left struggling in the sea. As the shells continued to fall around him, Khan swam 200 yards back to rescue his handler. Once they'd reached the shore he pulled him to solid ground, before collapsing next to him.

Khan was awarded the Dickin Medal for 'rescuing Corporal Muldoon from drowning under heavy shell fire'.

To date, there is only one cat who's been awarded the prestigious Dickin Medal – the highest British honour that can be given to an animal for bravery in battle. His name is Simon and his story dates back to more than seventy years ago, at the height of the Chinese Civil War.

The black and white tomcat was first discovered on the docks of Hong Kong in March 1948. At the time, China was in the midst of a conflict between Mao Tse Tung's People's Liberation Army (PLA) and the ruling nationalist (or Kuomintang) party of Chiang Kai-shek. The British sailor George Hickinbottom decided he'd be perfect for controlling the rodent population on the Royal Navy ship HMS *Amethyst*, so he smuggled him aboard.

A year later the ship sailed up the Yangtze River from Shanghai to Nanking to relieve the HMS *Consort* of its duties guarding the British Embassy. The British hadn't taken a side in the conflict, so no trouble was expected. However, when the *Amethyst* was about sixty miles from the city it was attacked by the communists who believed the British were invading Chinese waters.

Nineteen men, including the ship's captain, were killed and twenty-seven more wounded. The ship then entered the start of a three-month siege. On board conditions soon began to deteriorate. Many of the crew were traumatised by the loss of their crewmates and rations were cut in half as food and water supplies dwindled.

Simon suffered severe shrapnel wounds from the blast, but despite his injuries he still protected food stores from an infestation of rats that took hold. Within two months it was under control. His presence in the sick bay also helped keep up the morale of the crew.

As the siege reached its 101st day, negotiations were still at a stalemate. That evening, the captain saw an opportunity to escape up river to the open sea. It was successful, and within five hours the ship was cruising back to Hong Kong.

Simon was given a hero's welcome when the *Amethyst* returned to dock in Plymouth, and he became an international celebrity overnight, receiving fan mail and gift cans of food and cat toys. As well as being awarded the Dickin Medal, he was also given the rank of Able Seaman. However, Simon died in quarantine three weeks later. The crew were heartbroken and a plaque was unveiled on the ship in his memory.

It was 23 February 1942. A RAF bomber had just been shot down by enemy fire after returning from a mission over Norway. As it crashed into the North Sea, the crew on board realised there was little chance of survival. More than 100 miles from home and unable to radio back to their air base, the men faced almost certain death in freezing-cold waters. However, the crew were not entirely alone. On board was a blue chequered hen called Winkie. Carrier pigeons such as Winkie were routinely carried by bombers during World War II in the hope they could fly home to their lofts and alert colleagues back at their air base.

Just before the aircraft hit the water, the crew set the bird free in a last-ditch attempt to contact their rescuers. Incredibly, Winkie managed to fly the 120-mile journey back to her home in Broughty Ferry, near Dundee. By the time she was discovered by her owner George Ross, she was exhausted and covered in oil. He immediately contacted RAF Leuchars in Fife, who launched a rescue mission.

Although Winkie wasn't carrying a message, they were able to calculate the position of the aircraft through a number of different factors that included wind direction, her flight speed and the impact of the oil on her feathers. The men were found within fifteen minutes.

Winkie became an instant hero at the air base and a dinner was held in her honour. A year later she became the first animal to receive the Dickin Medal for 'delivering a message under exceptional circumstances'.

On every Dickin Medal there is an inscription that reads: 'We Also Serve'.

COURAGEOUS
CAMPAIGNERS

When 187 female workers walked out of a Ford factory in Dagenham over a pay dispute, the company's managers were hardly quaking in their boots. It was the summer of 1968 and the bra-burning wave of political feminism that had begun to sweep the US was yet to gain ground as an organised movement in the UK. However, the three-week strike was to become one of the most pivotal events in the history of the UK's women's liberation movement, highlighting women's rights and paving the way for the Equal Pay Act of 1970.

The women were sewing machinists, responsible for stitching the materials that made Ford's van and car seat covers. They were infuriated when they found out their role had been downgraded from 'more skilled' to 'less skilled' under a company restructure. This meant they would also be paid 15 per cent less than the full rate the men received within the 'less skilled' category. The women were in no doubt that the pay structure was blatantly unequal and leveraged in men's favour. But, importantly, it also revealed the managers had no recognition or respect for their skills.

A group of five women – Rose Boland, Eileen Pullen, Vera Sime, Gwen Davis, and Sheila Douglass – decided to lead the strike. They didn't have the full support of every one of their trade unionist representatives, or even the support of every woman on the shop floor. But on 7 June they were joined by more than 100 women as they walked out of the factory and made their way down the streets of London to demonstrate at the front of Westminster Hall. During the protest they unfurled a banner that said: 'We want sex equality'.

Without any car seat covers, Ford's assembly line came to a halt. Barbara Castle, the newly appointed Secretary of State for Employment and Productivity intervened. Within three weeks a deal was struck and the strike ended. The women's pay rate was increased to 8 per cent below that of men in the 'less skilled' category. It rose to the full amount the following year. However, their skill wasn't reinstated to its original category. It would take a further sixteen years, after a six-week strike by sewing machinists to be re-graded to 'more skilled' once again.

Inspired by the machinists, other women's labour and trade unionists founded the National Joint Action Campaign Committee for Women's Equal Rights (NJACCWER). On 18 May 1969, they held an equal pay demonstration in Trafalgar Square, which was attended by 1000 people.

In 1975, the Equal Pay Act of 1970 came into force, which aimed to eliminate discrimination between men and women. In parliament that day, the MP Shirley Summerskill praised the women machinists for the significant part they played in history in the struggle for equal pay.

OLIVE MORRIS

Olive Morris was born in 1952 in Harewood, St Catherine, Jamaica. She moved to south London at the age of nine with her family. When they arrived it was still commonplace to see signs in the windows of rental properties, buildings and public houses that prohibited black people from entering. And, at the time, it was completely legal for people to discriminate on the grounds of race. It would be another two years until the 1965 Race Relations Act outlawed racial discrimination in public places and made the promotion of hatred on the grounds of 'colour, race, or ethnic or national origins' an offence.

But a change in legislation didn't lead to an automatic change in attitudes within society or people who held authoritative powers. Olive left school in the late 1960s when tensions between the police and black community were escalating – not least for the sus laws that enabled police officers to stop and search people on mere suspicion that they'd committed a crime. Black people still faced discrimination in employment and housing. Attacks by the far right group the National Front were also on the increase.

After leaving school, Olive began to campaign against racial injustices, putting herself at great risk in the process. In 1969, she intervened in the brutal arrest of a Nigerian diplomat in Brixton – when she tried to stop the police beating him they turned on her. Olive was arrested and taken to a prison where she was beaten, verbally assaulted and threatened with rape. Her brother Basil could hardly recognise her after the attack.

In the early 1970s, she became a member of the youth section of the British Black Panther Movement. In 1974, she lived in a squat on Railton Road, Brixton with her friend Liz Obi. It was here that they founded the Brixton Black Women's Group (BWG) to address issues and challenges facing black women.

Throughout the 1970s, the BWG developed and transformed into the Black Women's Centre, relocating its premises to Stockwell Green. The squat became an organising centre for community groups such as Black People against State Harassment as well as housing Sabarr Bookshop, which was one of the first black community bookshops.

In 1975, Olive began a degree in Economics and Social Science at Manchester University, where she was involved in the work of the Manchester Black Women's Co-operative and the Black Women's Mutual Aid Group. She also campaigned for the abolition of fees for international students.

In 1978, she graduated and returned to Brixton. She, along with Stella Dadzie and other women, founded the Organisation of Women of African and Asian Descent (OWAAD). She also worked at the Brixton Community Law Centre where she campaigned for the scrapping of sus laws. A passionate writer, she was a strong advocate of dismantling institutionalised racism within the police and education system, as opposed to merely focusing on fighting fascism.

Later that year, Olive was diagnosed with Non-Hodgkin's lymphoma. She died in 1979, aged just twenty-seven. After the second wave of Brixton riots, in 1985, Lambeth Council named one of its key buildings after her.

In 2008, the Remembering Olive Collective (ROC) was started. Olive is also depicted on the one-pound denomination of the Brixton Pound, a local currency in that area of London. In 2011, the Olive Morris memorial award was launched to give bursaries to young black women who are engaged in grassroots political work.

> **AFTER LEAVING SCHOOL, OLIVE BEGAN TO CAMPAIGN AGAINST RACIAL INJUSTICES, PUTTING HERSELF AT GREAT RISK IN THE PROCESS. IN 1969, SHE INTERVENED IN THE BRUTAL ARREST OF A NIGERIAN DIPLOMAT IN BRIXTON – WHEN SHE TRIED TO STOP THE POLICE BEATING HIM THEY TURNED ON HER.**

In 1963, a group of black campaigners from Bristol organised a boycott that would revoke a company's colour bar and pave the way for the first legislation in the UK that outlawed racial discrimination. Inspired by the activism of Rosa Parks and other civil rights activists in the US, Paul Stephenson, Roy Hackett and Guy Bailey challenged, and overturned, the racist policies of the Bristol Omnibus Company.

Paul Stephenson was born in Rochford, Essex in 1937 to a British mother and West African father. He served in the Royal Air Force from 1953 to 1960 and gained a diploma in youth and community work in Birmingham. In 1962, he moved to Bristol to work as a youth officer for the council. He was determined to challenge the racism he'd encountered growing up and continued to face as a young man.

In the early 1960s, Bristol had an estimated 3000 citizens of West Indian origin. Some had served in the British military during both world wars. Others had emigrated to Britain after the war when the British government encouraged immigration from Commonwealth countries to help rebuild the country. A large majority worked in the NHS and public sector roles.

Despite this, they encountered discrimination in housing and employment, and experienced violence from gangs of white youths. Paul Stephenson joined the West Indian Association, an organisation that aimed to represent the community and tackle discrimination. They turned their attention to the nationalised Bristol Omnibus Company, who refused to employ black and Asian people on the bus crews. Local union officials from the Transport and General Workers' Union (TGWU) denied there was a colour bar. However, it transpired that the Passenger Group of the union had passed a resolution in 1955 that 'coloured workers' should not be employed on bus crews.

Paul Stephenson joined forces with an action group called the West Indian Development Council with four other West Indian men – Roy Hackett, Owen Henry, Audley Evans and Prince Brown. They set out to prove that the colour bar existed in the company by arranging an interview for Guy Bailey, an eighteen-year-old West Indian. He was well qualified for the vacancies that the company had advertised in the local paper just the day before.

However, when Guy turned up for the interview he was met with immediate hostility by the receptionist who informed the manager through the door of his office: 'Your two o'clock appointment is here, and he's black.' The manager refused to come out and face him. Instead he stated point blank: 'There's no point having an interview. We don't employ black people.'

On 29 April 1963, the group of activists announced a boycott of the bus network. Members of the local black community, supported by many of their white neighbours, refused to use the buses in protest.

Students from Bristol University also held a protest march to the bus station and the local headquarters of the TGWU on 1 May. The local MP Tony Benn contacted the then Labour opposition leader Harold Wilson, who spoke out against the colour bar at an Anti-Apartheid Movement rally in London. The boycott attracted national attention.

Paul Stephenson and the other campaigners were sidelined from negotiations between the unions and the bus company, which continued for several months. But on 28 August 1963, the general manager of the Bristol Omnibus Company announced that there would be no more discrimination in employing bus crews. It was on the same day that Martin Luther King made his famous 'I Have a Dream' speech at the March in Washington.

On 17 September, Raghbir Singh, a Sikh, became Bristol's first non-white bus conductor. A few days later two Jamaican and two Pakistani men joined him. It was a step in the right direction for racial equality. But there were still many racial injustices in the city and across the country to fight against. It was still legal to discriminate against people of colour in public places.

In 1964, Paul attracted national publicity again when he refused to leave a public house until he was served, resulting in a trial on a charge of failing to leave a licensed premises. The case was dismissed and the barman who'd refused to serve him was fired by his employers. In 1965, the United Kingdom Parliament passed a Race Relations Act, which made 'racial discrimination unlawful in public places'. This was followed by the Race Relations Act 1968 which extended the provisions to housing and employment.

In 2009, Paul was given an OBE 'for his services to equal opportunities and to community relations in Bristol'. Guy Bailey and Roy Hackett were also awarded OBEs for their important roles in the boycott and for fighting against racial inequality in society.

In August 2014, a plaque was unveiled inside Bristol Bus Station commemorating the bus boycott. In November 2017, Paul received a Pride of Britain Award for Lifetime Achievement. The judges said in his citation: 'He has changed the way we all live for the better, and his story reminds us that the battle for civil rights was not confined to America.'

In January 1968, tragedy struck the fishing community of Hull when several trawlers set off from the port of Kingston upon Hull. They were headed for the Arctic in search of their biggest catch yet. But before long they were facing one of the worst storms the fishermen had ever experienced, with waves up to forty feet high. Three of the boats sank and fifty-eight men lost their lives. Back in Hull, the mothers, wives, sisters and daughters the men had left behind gathered to grieve; one of the youngest widows was seventeen with two young children. They were devastated but also angry. Over the years, 6000 men from their community had died at sea.

One of the women, Lillian Bilocca – or 'Big Lil' as she would become known – decided to take on the trawler owners.

She would become a legendary figure in the community, demanding improvements to the health and safety of the industry, while changing attitudes towards the safety of men at sea, for good.

Hull had a longstanding connection to the fishing industry. By the 1960s, 150 deep-water trawlers were based at St Andrew's Dock and each year they brought in up to a quarter of a million tons of fish – 25 per cent of Britain's total catch. But the men who worked on the trawlers took huge risks to bring in these amounts, sailing 1000 miles away to Iceland. Health and safety procedures were almost non-existent and men were routinely lost overboard or killed by unsafe equipment. But the Triple Tragedy Disaster – as it became known – propelled the community into action.

Lillian worked as a cod skinner in a fish factory off the dock. She started a petition for better safety regulations at sea, which would develop into what became known as a Fishermen's Charter. Within ten days she had 10,000 signatures.

Lillian, along with 500 other women, marched to Victoria Hall in the city to demand action. She, along with Yvonne Blenkinsop who'd lost her father at sea four years earlier, spoke passionately to the press who had gathered outside. From there, they walked to St Andrew's Dock with 200 women to confront the owners of the trawlers. Mary Denness and Christine Jensen also helped lead the campaign, and together, the four of them became known as the Headscarf Revolutionaries. The women faced opposition from the trawler bosses, as well as some of the fishermen. But they were determined to improve safety measures.

Lililan and Yvonne travelled to London to meet with top

government ministers to demand radio operators aboard every ship, a mothership, and more modern materials. They also asked for restrictions to be placed on the use of inexperienced 'deckies' and a ban on fishing in bad weather. The government ordered an inquiry and summoned the trawler owners. Eighty-eight safety measures were enacted immediately. The women's successful campaign hit headlines around the world, but in the years that followed their community faced another tragedy as Hull's fishing industry fell into decline.

Today, the 'headscarf heroes' have been remembered with a plaque and a number of murals at the site of the old Victoria Hall on Hessle Road. In 2018, a BBC Four documentary – *Hull's Headscarf Heroes* – celebrating fifty years of the protest, revived interest in their story. That same year, a street in Hull was named after Lillian Bilocca.

MARK ASHTON

In 1984 a young activist Mark Ashton collected donations at the annual gay pride march in London, to support miners on strike. This led to the formation of the Lesbians and Gays Support the Miners (LGSM) group, which Mark co-founded with his friend Mike Jackson.

Mark was born in Oldham but he grew up in Portrush, County Antrim, Northern Ireland. He moved to London at the age of eighteen in the late 1970s. In 1982, he visited his parents in Bangladesh where his father was working for the textile machinery industry. While there, he witnessed extreme poverty. He returned to the UK a far more politicised creature and joined the Young Communist League.

He also volunteered for the London Lesbian and Gay Switchboard and supported the Campaign for Nuclear Disarmament. Mark could see parallels between the mining and gay community. Although on the surface the two groups appeared to have little in common, he believed they were both excluded from the political agenda as the police and government sought to marginalise and silence them. He saw just how dangerous this could prove to be, especially as a mysterious deadly virus began to take hold and infect high numbers of gay men in their community.

During the miners' strike, the government seized the funds of the National Union of Mineworkers (NUM). This meant there was no point in supporters sending donations to the union. The London LGSM group collected funds across the capital and soon conjoined with Neath, Dulais and Swansea Valleys support groups.

In December 1984, the group held a benefit concert – their largest fundraising event – in Camden. It was headlined by Jimmy Somerville. Together they raised around £22,500 for the miners and their families. This act of solidarity helped forge close ties between the LGBT community and British labour groups. But it also left a lasting legacy that ensured issues relating to the LGBT community were brought to the political agenda. In 1985, the Labour party passed a resolution in support of their commitment to LGBT rights. The miners' groups were some of the most vocal critics of Section 28 in the Local Government Act of 1988.

In 1987, Mark Ashton died from an AIDS-related illness. He was just twenty-six. In his memory, the Mark Ashton Trust was set up to raise money for individuals living with HIV.

**THIS ACT OF SOLIDARITY HELPED FORGE CLOSE
TIES BETWEEN THE LGBT COMMUNITY AND
BRITISH LABOUR GROUPS. BUT IT ALSO LEFT
A LASTING LEGACY THAT ENSURED ISSUES
RELATING TO THE LGBT COMMUNITY WERE
BROUGHT TO THE POLITICAL AGENDA.**

PRAGNA PATEL

Back in 1979, Pragna Patel became one of the founding
members of Southall Black Sisters (SBS). The organisation
was established in the aftermath of west London's race riots to
specifically address the needs of Black (Asian and African-
Caribbean) women. Since then it's consistently challenged
injustices in the legal and immigration system and won some
hard-fought and high-profile campaigns.

Pragna was five years old when she left Kenya with her
mother and younger sisters to join her father in Britain.
Throughout her school years she experienced a lot of racism
and struggled to find role models from her own background
that inspired any pride in her identity.

At the age of fourteen, Pragna began to read books about
Gandhi in the school library that improved her self-esteem
and helped to shape her ideology.

At seventeen she was almost forced into a marriage when
she was taken to a village in Gujarat, to meet a young man.
It was a pivotal moment for her. By the time she returned
to England she was engaged. But she refused point blank to
go through with the marriage, and continually repeated the

phrase, 'I will not submit' to her mother. Pragna had recently read James Joyce's *A Portrait of the Artist as a Young Man* and the words of its main character, Stephen Dedulus, had a profound effect on her.

Her mother grew increasingly exasperated but eventually gave up trying to persuade her daughter to marry. Pragna's persistence had paid off and she began to adopt the same attitude towards racism in society. In 1979, she helped set up the Southall Black Sisters organisation, which was formed in the aftermath of demonstrations against a National Front rally in the area. During the protests an anti-fascist campaigner, Blair Peach, was killed.

Pragna was inspired by many of the progressive activists she met through the organisation and the Law Centre movement, which provided legal aid to people who faced eviction or exploitation at work or school and couldn't afford to fight their cases. She left to attend college but returned in the early 1980s.

Since then, Southall Black Sisters has run many successful human rights campaigns, despite cuts to legal aid by successive governments. Over the years they have run many campaigns that highlight the specific problems that migrant women with insecure immigration status face. They've successfully repelled 'no recourse to public funds' and the one-year immigration rule that's trapped non-British women in violent marriages.

In 1992, the organisation achieved national acclaim when they helped overturn a life imprisonment sentence for a woman who'd killed her husband after suffering ten years of domestic abuse.

That same year, Pragna left the organisation to study and

train as a lawyer. But her growing awareness of the law's intrinsic bias regarding gender, race and class also encouraged her to return.

In 2010, the organisation was awarded Secularist of the Year by the National Secular Society, in recognition of their support of black and Asian women's human rights.

In 2011, Pragna was recognised in the *Guardian*'s Top 100 Women: Activists and Campaigners.

HEROES
OF WAR

SIMON WESTON

After four years of service in the British Army, Simon Weston suffered severe burns to his face and body when his ship was bombed by Argentine fighters during the Falklands War. Despite enduring years of physical pain and psychological trauma, Simon went on to help set up, and support, charities and foundations that help people with disfigurements.

Simon was just sixteen when he joined the Welsh Guards in 1978. After four years of service he was deployed to the Falkland Islands. On 8 June 1982, Simon was on board the RFA *Sir Galahad* in Port Pleasant near Fitzroy with other members of his platoon. They were just off the Falkland Islands when it was bombed by Argentine fighters during an air attack. The ship, which was carrying ammunition, phosphorous bombs and thousands of gallons of diesel and petrol was immediately set on fire.

The Welsh Guards lost forty-eight men in total and ninety-six were badly injured. Simon suffered 46 per cent burns. He was rushed to hospital at RAF Lyneham after the attack and only realised just how severe his injuries were when he passed his mother in the corridor. He called out to her and saw the look of horror on her face as she realised the severely burnt victim she didn't recognise was her own son.

Simon began years of reconstructive surgery, which included ninety-six major operations and surgical procedures. Surgeons took skin from his shoulders to make eyelids, and his nose was grafted on in a later operation. Simon started to drink heavily. Now that he was no longer a Welsh guardsman, he felt that he had no purpose in his life any more. He feared that he had nothing to offer and would never be accepted for the way he looked.

As he struggled to come to terms with his new reality, his mother reunited him with his old regiment. They encouraged him to stay positive and look ahead to the future, whatever that entailed.

In 1986, Simon received a letter from the Guards Association of Australasia asking him to go on a goodwill tour. It was his first time away from home since the incident and he was apprehensive about being away from his family. But he found that he enjoyed speaking about his experiences in public at charity dinners and events – something he'd never done before.

He was delighted when he discovered his appearances had resulted in people donating to a children's burns unit. For the first time since he'd been injured, he felt useful again. Inspired by a new-found sense of purpose, Simon became a patron for a number of charities that supported people living with disfigurements. He also became lead ambassador for the Healing Foundation Centre, which funds new advances in the prevention and treatment of children's burns.

Over the years, Simon has also campaigned for adequate healthcare, support and compensation for British troops and veterans. In 2000 he met and became friends with First Lieutenant Carlos Cachon, the Argentine pilot who dropped the bomb and caused his injuries. Married with three children, in 2016, he was awarded a CBE for his service to charities.

FOR THE FIRST TIME SINCE HE'D BEEN INJURED, HE FELT USEFUL AGAIN. INSPIRED BY A NEW-FOUND SENSE OF PURPOSE, SIMON BECAME A PATRON FOR A NUMBER OF CHARITIES THAT SUPPORTED PEOPLE LIVING WITH DISFIGUREMENTS.

PIONEERING WOMEN

CICELY SAUNDERS

Once described as 'the woman who changed the face of death', Cicely Saunders held a deep-seated conviction that terminally ill people could live with dignity, and without pain. Her beliefs spearheaded the modern hospice movement and helped to revolutionise palliative care.

In 1938, Cicely started studying at Oxford University, but at the outbreak of World War II she left to train as a nurse in London. During her training, she saw a great need to improve the quality of life for patients who were suffering a terminal illness. However, due to a back injury she went on to qualify as a medical social worker.

In 1948, she forged a close friendship with a Polish Jewish refugee David Tasma when she was based at Archway Hospital. He was dying of cancer and had only six months to live. Together, they created a vision for a hospice that provided psychological and spiritual support, in addition to physical care. David left her £500 in his will to turn their dream into a reality.

Cicely founded St Christopher's Hospice in 1967. It was the world's first hospice to combine pain and symptom relief with holistic care, which was focused on the individual needs of patients and their family. It was designed to be a 'home from home' with beautiful gardens and light, bright spaces to enjoy. Patients were invited to take part in a wide range of activities that included gardening, art classes or having their hair styled. The hospice's aim to celebrate life was underpinned by a care philosophy that 'you matter because you are you. And you matter till the last moment of your life.'

In 1979, Cicely was appointed Dame Commander of the Order of the British Empire (DBE). In 2001, St Christopher's received the world's largest humanitarian award, the Conrad N. Hilton Humanitarian Prize.

CHI-CHI NWANOKU

In 2005, classical musician Chi-chi Nwanoku was introduced to the work of eighteenth-century composer Joseph Bologne, Chevalier de Saint-Georges. The composer was born in 1745, the son of a wealthy French plantation owner and his wife's African slave of Senegalese origin. However, although his body of work included three operas, two symphonies and twelve concertos, Chi-chi had never heard of him. As she looked back into the archives she began to discover even more composers of colour who'd been excluded from the classical cannon. This prompted her to found the Chineke! Foundation and Europe's first professional orchestra made up of black and minority ethnic musicians.

Chi-chi was born in 1956 in Fulham, London. She is of Nigerian and Irish descent. Chi-chi began playing piano at the age of seven. She was a talented sprinter, as well as musician, but had to end her athletic career following a knee injury. It was this that made her pick up the double bass at eighteen and actively pursue a career in music. Chi-chi went on to study at the Royal Academy of Music where she was the only black student. After graduating, she was soon in international demand as a musician.

In 2015, Chi-chi founded the Chineke! Foundation, which supports, inspires and encourages Black and Minority Ethnic classical musicians working in the UK and Europe. The organisation aims to increase representation of black and minority ethnic musicians in British and European orchestras, and gives them a platform to excel though the Chineke! Orchestra. The foundation also created a junior orchestra for players up to eighteen, as well as an annual competition and a mentoring programme.

In the same year, Chi-chi also presented the BBC Radio 4 programme *In Search of the Black Mozart*. It featured the lives and careers of black classical composers and performers from the eighteenth century, which included

Joseph Bologne, Chevalier de Saint-Georges, Ignatius Sancho, and George Bridgetower.

The Chineke! Orchestra, made up of sixty-two musicians representing thirty-one different nationalities, first performed in 2015 at the Queen Elizabeth Hall. Since then, their reputation has grown and they've been in constant demand, performing almost every month.

In 2017, Chi-chi was awarded Officer of the Order of the British Empire for services to music. In addition, she has been made an Honorary Fellow of both the Royal Academy of Music and Trinity Laban Conservatoire of Music.

In 2018 the BBC *Woman's Hour* placed Chi-chi ninth in a list of the world's most powerful women in music. She was also listed in the 2019 and 2020 Power List of the most influential Black Britons of the year.

IN 2018 THE BBC *WOMAN'S HOUR* PLACED CHI-CHI NINTH IN A LIST OF THE WORLD'S MOST POWERFUL WOMEN IN MUSIC. SHE WAS ALSO LISTED IN THE 2019 AND 2020 POWER LIST OF THE MOST INFLUENTIAL BLACK BRITONS OF THE YEAR.

MARGARET BUSBY

In 1967, Margaret Busby co-founded the publishing company Allison & Busby. She was Britain's youngest and first black woman book publisher.

Margaret was born in 1944 in Accra, Gold Coast (present-day Ghana) to parents who had roots in Barbados, Trinidad and Dominica. She and her sister were sent to an international boarding school in Sussex. Margaret received what she described as a 'thoroughly English education'. But at no point throughout her education, either at school or London University, where she studied English, did she come into contact with a single book written by an African.

The absence of any explanation in literary form to her presence in Britain, or the UK's history with Africa, troubled her. It was as though her identity had been erased. Margaret began to seek out writers that referenced her continent and African people. It was a life-changing experience for Margaret to discover writers that included Chinua Achebe and Flora Nwapa in the African Writers Series, initiated by Heinemann Educational Books.

She met her future business partner Clive Allison at an undergraduate party, where they came up with the idea of starting their own publishing company. The first novel they took on was *The Spook Who Sat by the Door* by Sam Greenlee, which been rejected on both sides of the Atlantic. It was published in March 1969 to critical acclaim and is regarded as inspiring the Blaxploitation genre of films in the 1970s.

Margaret went on to become A&B's editorial director for twenty years. Though A&B did not exclusively publish Black authors, it brought the work of several writers from the African diaspora to the public's attention, such as Buchi Emecheta, C.L.R. James and George Lamming.

In 1992 Margaret compiled *Daughters of Africa: An International Anthology of Words and Writings by Women*

of African Descent from the Ancient Egyptian to the Present.
It was described by Black Enterprise as 'a landmark', and
includes contributions in a range of genres by more than
200 women.

Margaret was appointed OBE for services to literature
and publishing in 2006. In 2019, she was presented with the
inaugural Lifetime Achievement in African Literature award
during the Africa Writes festival in London.

LAURA BATES

In April 2012, Laura Bates founded the Everyday Sexism
project to highlight and challenge incidences of harassment
and sexism that women experience on a daily basis in society.
By April 2015, the website had reached 100,000 entries.

Laura was awarded the British Empire Medal in the 2015
Birthday Honours for services to gender equality. Her first
book, *Everyday Sexism*, was shortlisted for Waterstones Book
of the Year. In 2018 Laura was elected Fellow of the Royal
Society of Literature in its '40 Under 40' initiative.

HEROES IN THE MIDST OF TERROR

ABERFAN HEROES

On a cold morning in late October 1966, a teacher from Aberfan led her pupils to safety after their primary school was engulfed by an avalanche of waste from the nearby colliery tip. The disaster claimed the lives of 28 adults and 116 children and the village would be forever overshadowed by the tragedy. Hettie Williams is just one of a number of teachers remembered and honoured in the village for their calm and quick-thinking actions that saved children's lives that day.

Events leading up to the disaster go back to the nineteenth century, when Merthyr Vale Colliery was opened in 1869. The first coal was produced in 1875. By 1916 the colliery had run out of space to tip the waste that coal mining produced. It began to tip on the mountains above the village of Aberfan.

By the time of the disaster there were seven tips on the hills, though only one was in use. These tips consisted of waste rock and soil – or 'spoil' as it was known – and contained fine particles of ash.

Since the nationalisation of the British coal industry in 1947, Aberfan's colliery had been under the control of the National Coal Board (NCB). By 1966 the village's population had grown to 5000 and the majority of people who lived there were employed in the coal industry.

The stability of the tips was affected by streams and springs on the hillside and weather conditions. Between 1952 and 1965 Aberfan was affected by significantly high rainfall, which resulted in severe flooding in the village. Several of the tips had also suffered minor slips. Residents made several complaints to The Merthyr Tydfil County Borough Council, who liaised their concerns to the NCB regarding the danger that the coal slurry posed to Pantglas junior and secondary schools, which were at the bottom of the hillside. In early 1965 the council and NCB held meetings to address the problems that had caused the flooding. But no further action was taken. By the time of the disaster, the tip that was still in use stood at 111 feet high, at the top of the mountain.

In the first three weeks of October 1966, 6½ inches of rain fell in the village. On the morning of 21 October at around 7.30, one of the colliery's workers reported that one of the tips had slipped by ten feet. At 9.15am, 150,000 tonnes of liquified waste broke away from the tip. It flowed 700 yards down the mountain destroying everything in its wake including two farm cottages and eighteen houses. It raced on towards the village at a speed of up to 21 miles per hour in waves that reached up to 30 feet.

Survivors of the disaster remember the sound of a deafening roar that would remain with them for the rest of their lives. Hettie – Miss Taylor at the time – was twenty-three years old and had just started a lesson with her class of pupils aged between seven and eight. They were more excitable than usual. That afternoon they were due to break up for the half-term holiday. When Hettie first heard the sound she told the children to get under their desks and stay calm.

As the avalanche struck the school, the entire building shook and cracks appeared across the wall behind Hettie's desk. The light shades swung and jangled from the force of the hit. The school had been buried under the waste tip, but Hettie spotted a gap in the classroom for her pupils to escape through. She told them to get out from under their desks, walk straight out into the yard and not to look back.

Thousands of volunteers arrived in the village to help with the rescue mission. They managed to find twenty-eight children in the rubble, who survived. But no survivors were found after 11am. Out of the 116 children killed, the majority were aged between seven and ten.

After the disaster, Hettie helped set up a school, with three other surviving teachers, at the local community centre. In August 2018 Hettie died at the age of seventy-five. Hundreds came to pay their respects at her funeral, including some of the pupils she saved that day.

David Davies, chairman of the Aberfan Memorial Charity, added: 'The people of Aberfan will never forget our dear Hettie.'

Rennie Williams was just one of four teachers to survive

the disaster, along with Hettie, Mair Morgan and Howell Williams. She had just taken the register when she heard a sudden crashing sound. She immediately rushed to the school hall and put her own life at risk to rescue children who were trapped in the rubble.

Over the years Rennie continued to stay in touch with the children, many of who suffered post-traumatic stress. Jeff Edwards was just eight years old when she rescued him. He attended her funeral to pay his respects when she died in May 2020, although he was saddened that many more couldn't attend due to coronavirus restrictions.

Nansi Williams, a dinner lady at the school, didn't survive the disaster but she saved the lives of five children that day. Two minutes before the building was struck, Nansi was collecting dinner money from the pupils in a corridor. As the school shook and smashed-in glass flew towards them, she told the children to get on the ground. She flung herself on top of them and took the full impact of a wall that crushed them together. Nansi was killed instantly.

Karen Thomas was one of the children she shielded who was found alive underneath Nansi's body. She remembers shouting at Nansi and pulling her hair after they were buried in the rubble, trying to get a response from her. Karen visits Nansi's grave every year on the anniversary of the disaster to thank her and lay flowers.

On 26 October that year, 1966, a tribunal was set up to inquire into the causes of the disaster. The report found that it could and should have been prevented.

Today, the Aberfan memorial garden and cemetery remember the 144 people who died in the disaster.

TWO MINUTES BEFORE THE BUILDING WAS STRUCK, NANSI WAS COLLECTING DINNER MONEY FROM THE PUPILS IN A CORRIDOR. AS THE SCHOOL SHOOK AND SMASHED-IN GLASS FLEW TOWARDS THEM, SHE TOLD THE CHILDREN TO GET ON THE GROUND. SHE FLUNG HERSELF ON TOP OF THEM AND TOOK THE FULL IMPACT OF A WALL THAT CRUSHED THEM TOGETHER.

HILLSBOROUGH DISASTER

In 1989, eight-year-old Joe Smith was saved from the crush at Hillsborough Stadium by a stranger who pulled him out of the crowd and hoisted him onto his shoulders. Twenty-seven years later Joe met John McMahon, the man who'd saved him, to thank him personally.

They were just two of thousands of Liverpool FC fans who flocked to Hillsborough, Sheffield Wednesday's home ground, on 15 April 1989 for the FA Cup semi-final between Liverpool and Nottingham Forest. The match had sold out and the game was due to kick-off at 3pm. But events that day would lead to the deaths of ninety-six Liverpool fans and change the way that stadium football games were played for ever.

It was a combination of defects in the stadium's design and police errors that led to the fatal crush of thousands of Liverpool supporters. At the time it was common practice for terraces to be divided into pens by high fences that separated fans from the pitch. That day, there was no proper system in place to ensure fans were evenly distributed in the six front pens. There also weren't enough turnstiles to ensure that fans could enter the ground in steady or safe numbers.

Half an hour before the game was due to start, there were still thousands of supporters attempting to enter the Leppings Lane end of the stadium. This caused severe crushing in the two central pens, which were already full. As the game kicked off, fans were pressed up against the crush barriers.

As one of the pens gave way, people began to collapse onto the pitch. Some supporters managed to climb the fence to escape while others were helped to safety by people in the upper tiers of the stadium. John, who was sixteen at the time, managed to escape over the fence, but once he'd got to safety he looked back and spotted Joe surrounded by the crowd in the pen. He grabbed him and pulled him out from the chaos. He then reunited him with his stepfather who had lost him in the crowd. John returned to the pen to help other people who were still trapped. Many fans were hauled out of the pens and treated for asphyxia on the pitch.

At 15:05 the referee stopped play. At 15:21 a senior ambulance station officer declared Hillsborough a major incident.

Joe and John didn't see each other for another twenty-seven years. It wasn't until a video went viral, revealing previously unseen footage of John's courageous act, that Joe was able to trace him.

John has always dismissed that he acted like a hero that day, stating that he helped where he could, just as many other hundreds of Liverpool supporters were. Supporters such as Dr Glyn Phillips, an off-duty GP. He was in one of the central pens with his brother and two friends. When the match was stopped, Dr Glyn climbed into the other pen and tried to jump over the fence. In the process he banged his head on the crossbar and started bleeding. Despite this he ran onto the pitch to help eighteen-year-old Gary Currie, who wasn't breathing. With the help of a nurse he began to perform CPR and after ten to fifteen minutes, Gary's pulse returned. Glyn continued to give mouth to mouth as he carried him to an ambulance before going back on the pitch to help others. He later found out that he'd saved Gary's life.

Frederick Eccleston was a senior nursing manager who'd supported Liverpool FC for over forty years. When he realised a crush was happening he left the north-west terrace and went onto the pitch to help pull people through the gate in the pitch perimeter fence. He also gave first aid to a number of injured fans and tried to resuscitate another.

Ambulance driver Andrew Lawson was working a second job in the restaurant in the south stand of the stadium. When he saw fans climbing out of the pens he helped St John Ambulance volunteers give CPR to a teenage boy. After a minute and a half his pulse returned. He also went to phone an ambulance to report a major incident as he knew they needed a lot more help.

Stuart Gray was the general manager of Kidderminster and District Health Authority when he attended the match. During the crush he passed out in one of the pens. When he regained consciousness he saw a young man collapsed at his feet. It was eighteen-year-old John McBride. Stuart cleared his airway and performed mouth to mouth and CPR. Sadly, he was unable to revive John.

For twenty-seven years the families of the victims fought a long, hard battle to uncover the truth behind what led to the deaths of their loved ones. Finally, in April 2016, a jury at the

Great British Spirit

Hillsborough inquests ruled that the ninety-six victims were unlawfully killed.

The disaster led to a number of safety improvements in the largest English football grounds – fenced standing terraces were removed in favour of all-seater stadiums.

In April 1999, a memorial was unveiled at Hillsborough stadium, on the tenth anniversary of the disaster. It reads: 'In memory of the ninety-six men, women, and children who tragically died and the countless people whose lives were changed for ever. FA Cup semi-final Liverpool v Nottingham Forest. 15 April 1989. "You'll never walk alone".'

IN THE PROCESS HE BANGED HIS HEAD ON THE CROSSBAR AND STARTED BLEEDING. DESPITE THIS HE RAN ONTO THE PITCH TO HELP EIGHTEEN-YEAR-OLD GARY CURRIE, WHO WASN'T BREATHING. WITH THE HELP OF A NURSE HE BEGAN TO PERFORM CPR AND AFTER TEN TO FIFTEEN MINUTES, GARY'S PULSE RETURNED.

ACTS OF
BRAVERY

CAPTAIN OATES

Explorer Captain Lawrence Oates committed the ultimate sacrifice when he walked out into a blizzard in 1912, during the Terra Nova expedition to the Antarctic, rather than compromise his team's chances of survival.

Lawrence was born in 1880, in London. His uncle was the explorer Frank Oates. In 1898, Lawrence joined the West Yorkshire regiment and served during the Boer War as a junior officer in 1900. He was recommended for the Victoria Cross for his actions during operations in the Transvaal, the Orange River Colony, and Cape Colony. After peace was declared, Lawrence returned to England. In 1906, he was promoted to captain and served in Ireland, Egypt and India.

In 1910, he was accepted to join Robert Falcon Scott's Terra Nova expedition, officially the British Antarctic Expedition, to the South Pole. He was nicknamed 'the soldier' and was tasked with looking after nineteen ponies that Scott intended to use for sledge hauling. Their suitability for the job was a bone of contention between the two men – Lawrence believed the ponies were 'too old' for the task, and was eventually proved right – but Scott praised Lawrence's expert handling of the animals, which was fundamental to increasing the team's chances of success.

On 1 November 1911, Lawrence took off for the South Pole from their base camp in Cape Evans with fourteen other members of the expedition. At different points of the 895-mile journey, the support members of the expedition were sent back in teams. It became increasingly obvious that the ponies chosen weren't suitable for the job, something Lawrence had initially feared.

On 4 January 1912, three people remained with Scott and Lawrence to march the last 167 miles to the Pole – Edward Wilson, Henry Bowers and Edgar Evans. They reached the Pole – seventeen days later. However, they discovered they'd been beaten by the Norwegian explorer Roald Amundsen and his team, who'd arrived thirty-five days before. The men began a very difficult journey back home enduring freezing cold temperatures, sustained injuries from falls and ever-dwindling food supplies. On 17 February, Edgar died. Lawrence's feet were severely frostbitten and his weakened state was causing the rest of the party to fall behind schedule.

On 16 March, Lawrence walked out of his tent into a minus-40-degree blizzard. According to Robert Scott's diary, his last words were: 'I am just going outside and may be some time.' Lawrence didn't return.

The remaining three carried on for a further twenty miles but died nine days later. Their frozen bodies were found later that year by a search party. Lawrence's body was never found.

A cairn and cross were erected near the spot where

Lawrence was presumed to have died. It bore the inscription: 'Hereabouts died a very gallant gentleman, Captain L. E. G. Oates, of the Inniskilling Dragoons. In March 1912, returning from the Pole, he walked willingly to his death in a blizzard, to try and save his comrades, beset by hardships.'

BARBARA JANE HARRISON

British flight attendant Barbara Jane Harrison is the only woman to be awarded the George Cross for bravery in peacetime. She was just twenty-two when she died evacuating people from a blaze on board an aeroplane at Heathrow Airport.

Barbara was born in 1945 in Bradford, West Yorkshire. Her family later moved to Scarborough and Doncaster, where Barbara attended school until 1962. After leaving she worked at Martins Bank until 1964 before taking several jobs as a nanny in Switzerland and San Francisco.

In May 1966, Barbara joined British Overseas Airways Corporation (BOAC) as a flight attendant. After completing her training she was assigned to work on their Boeing 707 fleet. She moved to Kensington, London, where she shared a flat with other flight attendants.

On 8 April 1968, Barbara was on board BOAC Flight 712 when it left Heathrow Airport at 16:27, bound for Sydney. Almost immediately after take-off, a major fire developed in one of the engines and the plane returned to the airport for an emergency landing. One of the officers on the flight, John Hutchinson, remembers the fuel tank exploding and the fire spreading from the tail of the aeroplane up to the main body of the aircraft.

Barbara immediately followed evacuation procedures. She opened the rear door, inflated the escape chute and began to help passengers evacuate from the rear of the aircraft. She did this on her own as one of her colleagues jumped off to untwist the chute and was unable to get back on to the aircraft to help her. She encouraged some passengers to jump and pushed out others.

While some stewards left by emergency chutes to help extinguish the fire, Barbara continued to stay at the back of the plane and help passengers to safety. As it became impossible to escape from the tail end of the plane, due to continual explosions, she directed passengers to another exit.

As Barbara prepared to jump from the plane, smoke and flames engulfed her. But it is thought she turned back inside to help rescue four more passengers, which included an eight-year-old girl and a disabled elderly passenger. None of them survived. Their bodies were found by the rear door; they died from asphyxia. All the other passengers on board survived.

In August 1969, Barbara became the only woman to receive the George Cross in peacetime, and is the youngest female recipient of the medal. It is now at British Airways' Speedbird Centre, which is dedicated to the history of the crew and the story of BA.

In 1968, The Barbara Harrison Prize was established by the Royal Air Force Institute of Aviation Medicine. And since 2010, the Barbara Harrison Memorial Prize is awarded to the student of the Diploma in Aviation Medicine Course 'who has demonstrated commitment to others and determination to succeed through the course and in gaining the diploma'.

In 2019, a blue plaque was unveiled to honour Barbara at Bradford City Hall in Centenary Square. British Airways paid for the blue plaque for the people of Bradford. It is now permanently sited on the wall outside her former home.

Si Cunningham, from Bradford Civic Society, said: 'Her remarkable act of bravery must never be forgotten. She is regarded as a truly great Bradfordian and someone we are all immensely proud of.'

TERRY WAITE

In 1987 Terry Waite travelled to Lebanon on behalf of the Church of England to secure the release of four hostages. While there, he was kidnapped and held captive until 1991. Despite suffering four years of physical and mental torture he returned twenty-five years later to make peace with, and forgive, his captors.

In the late 1960s and 70s, Terry travelled extensively in East Africa and Europe with his wife and four children, narrowly escaping death on several occasions during the Idi Amin coup in Uganda. It was there he founded the Southern Sudan Project, which was responsible for the development of the region, and worked on a variety of programmes that advised on inter-cultural relations and health and education.

In 1978, Terry returned to the UK where he began working for the British Council of Churches. Throughout the early 1980s he successfully negotiated the release of a number of hostages including four that were captured in Libya. On 12 January 1987 he arrived in Beirut as the special envoy of the then Archbishop of Canterbury, intending to negotiate with the Islamic Jihad Organisation, for the release of American hostages Lawrence Jenco and David Jacobsen. He was promised safe conduct to visit them, but the group accused him of being a CIA agent and took him hostage instead.

Terry was held captive for 1763 days. For the first year he was kept in solitary confinement and chained to a radiator for twenty-three hours a day. He was routinely beaten, tortured and subjected to mock executions, but he refused to give up on the hope of being released. As he lay in his cell, he learnt to live one day at time and began to write a book in his head that would become an international bestseller years later. He also drew on the hymns, psalms and prayers he'd learnt as a chorister in his youth, for comfort.

Terry was released in November 1991. He decided to devote his life to writing, lecturing and humanitarian activities. His book, *Taken on Trust*, was published in 1995. In 2004, he founded the charity Hostage UK that aims to support families of hostages. He is patron to many others, including Able Child Africa and Habitat for Humanity.

In 2012, Terry returned to Beirut to meet and reconcile with representatives of the organisations that were responsible for his capture. It was the first time he'd been there since he was captured in 1991 and he knew the visit wasn't without its risks.

He said: 'I met with them quite prepared to put my own sufferings in the past. The only way forward is by the pathway of forgiveness, which is a difficult and dangerous road.'

MARK TAYLOR

In April 1999, David Copeland, a former member of the British National Party and the National Socialist Movement, coordinated a series of nail bomb attacks throughout the city of London – Electric Avenue in Brixton, Brick Lane in the East End, and a pub in the Soho. The latter was aimed at the heart of London's gay community.

It was a crowded Friday night ahead of the Bank Holiday weekend. Manager Mark Taylor was gearing up for one of the busiest evenings of the year at his pub, the Admiral Duncan, on Old Compton Street. He was also on the lookout for anything suspicious. He'd been briefed by police about a possible bomb threat and had been on a training course to deal with such a situation only a week before.

At around 6.30pm customers spotted an unattended sports bag inside the pub. Mark told customers to move away while he investigated, acting as a human shield. As he bent over to inspect the bag the bomb exploded. Almost 75 per cent of his body suffered severe burns. A three-inch nail was embedded in his left elbow, as well as a large shard of metal in his right calf.

Mark recovered in St Thomas's hospital in London for four weeks and received specialist treatment at a burns unit in West Sussex. Hundreds of people wrote letters of support and thanks to him, including singer Diana Ross.

Three people were killed, including a pregnant woman. The Admiral Duncan reopened its doors nine weeks later at exactly 18.37, the precise moment the bomb explosion had taken place. Hundreds gathered outside the bar for a ceremony to honour the victims. A light with three candles and eighty-six bulbs was included in the refurbishment, as a tribute to the dead and injured.

CONCORDIA DISASTER

On the night of 13 January 2012, the Italian cruise ship *Costa Concordia* struck an underwater rock off Isola del Giglio in the Mediterranean. On board were 1023 crewmembers and 3206 passengers.

Nineteen-year-old James Thomas, from Birmingham, was chatting to his girlfriend online when he was flung from his bed by the force of the impact. He'd been working as a dancer for six months. The ship plunged into darkness and started to shake.

Although an initial announcement stated this was due to a technical fault, James knew it was more serious than that. He was right. Shortly after, the signal was given to abandon ship.

James made his way to one of the emergency points. But a 53-metre tear in the ship's port side had caused irreparable damage. The ship was already tilting to such an extreme degree it was impossible to follow normal evacuation procedures. Panic ensued. James recalls: 'It became a fight for your life, basically.'

At this point, the ship resembled a water slide. But James managed to stay calm and began to slide his way through the centre of the ship towards the life rafts, hauling himself up onto furniture that was still fortunately fixed to the floor. In the process he helped around ten passengers reach the other side of the ship. However, they soon realised they were unable to reach the deck where the lifeboats were situated because the drop was too far. By this point, they were knee-deep in water.

But James's height and quick thinking turned a desperate and frightening situation around. At 6ft 3in, he bridged the gap between the two decks, using his body as a human ladder. He lowered himself into position and grabbed the lifeboat with one arm and the rail of the upper deck with his other. More than a dozen passengers, including a man and his disabled wife, climbed down his shoulder and body to safety. James turned back to help more passengers but was pulled into a lifeboat by one of the men he'd helped.

The ship's captain, Francesco Schettino, was found guilty of manslaughter in connection with the disaster and sentenced to sixteen years in prison. Although more than 4,200 people were rescued, thirty-two died.

THAILAND CAVE RESCUE

In the summer of 2018, John Volanthen and Richard Stanton received a call to rescue a group of schoolchildren trapped in a cave in Thailand. It was feared there was little chance of finding them alive. The men were experienced cavers who specialised in rescue operations through the British Cave Rescue Council, but these were exceptional circumstances.

The twelve young Thai footballers (aged between eleven

and seventeen) had been exploring with their coach in a cave system in Tham Luang, in the Chiang Rai province. A sudden heavy storm had flooded the entrance with heavy rain and they'd been forced deeper into the cave. By the time the British Cave Rescue Council was contacted, the boys had been trapped for over a week without food or light.

The cave's caverns and crevices posed extreme difficulties for rescuers. The death of an experienced former Thai navy diver during one rescue operation highlighted just how dangerous the mission was.

On 2 July, John and Richard ventured into the caves. The rescue mission included more than 100 divers and 10,000 people. John was one of the first to reach the boys and their coach. After winding his way through a series of passages he was overjoyed to find them all alive on an elevated rock, about two and a half miles from the cave entrance.

However, they now had to find a way to take the boys to safety. The organisers discussed different options – from drilling or finding a new entrance, to waiting for the floodwaters to subside. But with more heavy rain forecast there was the risk of water levels rising even further. The team spent the next five days pumping water from the cave. However, as water continued to flow in from streams and sinkholes in the hills above, they realised they were in a race against time. There was also the difficult task of building up the boys' strength and morale. While they prepared their rescue operation, divers took lighting into the cave and delivered much-needed food and medical supplies. They also played chess with the boys and brought letters from their parents.

On 8 July, the rescue team fitted the boys with full-face

breathing masks. One by one they were strapped to a rescue diver and guided out through dark and tight passageways. After they made their way through the flooded section, the boys were carried along ropes on stretchers before they reached the entrance of the cage. The group were located at least 800 metres below the surface of the cave and each journey to and from the entrance took at least two hours.

By the 10th, all twelve of the boys and their coach had been rescued and transported to hospital.

John and Richard were greeted by Thai ministers for Tourism and Travel as they boarded their flight back home to the UK. They were awarded free travel to the country – for life.

John was awarded a George Medal for 'great courage'. As a Cub leader, he was also awarded the Bronze Cross – the Scout Associations' highest honour, given for 'heroism or action in the face of extraordinary risk'. He was 'very humbled' and said knowing that all the children survived was his 'biggest reward'.

AFTER THEY MADE THEIR WAY THROUGH THE FLOODED SECTION, THE BOYS WERE CARRIED ALONG ROPES ON STRETCHERS BEFORE THEY REACHED THE ENTRANCE OF THE CAGE. THE GROUP WERE LOCATED AT LEAST 800 METRES BELOW THE SURFACE OF THE CAVE AND EACH JOURNEY TO AND FROM THE ENTRANCE TOOK AT LEAST TWO HOURS.

INDIVIDUAL ACTS OF KINDNESS

♦ DREAMFLIGHT

Back in 1986, British cabin crew member Patricia Pearce helped to organise Skyride – a British Airways initiative that took underprivileged children on a one-hour Christmas party flight. It inspired her to raise money to take children with a serious illness or disability to Walt Disney World in Florida.

Patricia co-founded Dreamflight with Derek Pereira, who also worked for BA. Their aim was to help increase the children's confidence and sense of independence – for the majority of the children it would be their first holiday without their parents. However, they realised this wouldn't be possible without twenty-four-hour support and care for the children. Patricia and Derek began to fundraise and recruit volunteer doctors, nurses and physiotherapists from all around the UK.

In November 1987, the first trip took place. Since then, 192 children, aged between eight and eleven, have flown to

Orlando each year for a one-off trip that would have been impossible otherwise.

Many children who return from the trip feel more confident in their ability to take on new challenges. Paralympic gold-medal swimmer and Dreamflight patron, Liz Johnson, is just one of the children who benefitted from the transformative effect of the holiday. As an eleven-year-old girl with cerebral palsy, the experience helped give her the confidence to follow her dream of becoming an Olympic athlete.

In 2008, eight of the returning Paralympians from Beijing – many of them medal-winning – had been Dreamflight children and cited the trip as a turning point for them.

'Beyond Dreamflight' was also set up to give children the opportunity to build on their self-confidence, and develop their independence, by providing extra support and help for their specific needs upon their return.

Patricia was awarded an MBE in 1997 and carried the Olympic torch in 2012.

MANY CHILDREN WHO RETURN FROM THE TRIP FEEL MORE CONFIDENT IN THEIR ABILITY TO TAKE ON NEW CHALLENGES. PARALYMPIC GOLD-MEDAL SWIMMER AND DREAMFLIGHT PATRON, LIZ JOHNSON, IS JUST ONE OF THE CHILDREN WHO BENEFITTED FROM THE TRANSFORMATIVE EFFECT OF THE HOLIDAY. AS AN ELEVEN-YEAR-OLD GIRL WITH CEREBRAL PALSY, THE EXPERIENCE HELPED GIVE HER THE CONFIDENCE TO FOLLOW HER DREAM OF BECOMING AN OLYMPIC ATHLETE.

NICK GIBSON

Every year, on Valentine's Day, the owner of The Drapers Arms in Islington, north London, donates all of the pub's takings that day to Refuge, a charity that supports women and children experiencing domestic violence.

As the owner of a pub that serves the heart of north London, Nick Gibson was motivated by a desire to do something significant that would help people in his community. But the annual donation is also a gesture of solidarity to thousands of women and children across the country who are victims of domestic violence. The charity's specialist services include refuges, community outreach and a twenty-four-hour helpline.

Since 2013, Nick has donated every single penny of his Valentine's takings. In 2016 he gave more than £10,000 to Refuge, when he had one of his most successful Valentine's ever.

In January 2015, a disabled pensioner was attacked and knocked to the ground outside his home in Low Fell, Gateshead. Alan Barnes, sixty-seven, suffered a broken collarbone and was too distressed to return home. Katie Cutler, a twenty-two-year-old beautician, also from Gateshead, read about his ordeal in a newspaper and felt compelled to help him. She set up a fundraising page on Go Fund Me and urged people to donate towards the cost of relocating him to new accommodation, where he would feel safe. 'We can't take away what has happened but with a little donation we can make the future a prettier one and help towards the cost of his new home.'

Katie's original fundraising target was £500. But within only a week she'd received over £330,000. Donations came in from countries around the world – New Zealand, USA, South Africa and Canada.

While Alan continued to recover from the attack, he was overwhelmed and heartened by the public's generosity, which helped to restore his faith in humanity. The donations meant that he could buy a house of his own for the first time. Alan also received offers of help from local tradesmen and removal services.

Later that year, Katie was awarded a British Empire Medal for services to fundraising in the community of Gateshead.

KATIE'S ORIGINAL FUNDRAISING TARGET WAS £500. BUT WITHIN ONLY A WEEK SHE'D RECEIVED OVER £330,000. DONATIONS CAME IN FROM COUNTRIES AROUND THE WORLD – NEW ZEALAND, USA, SOUTH AFRICA AND CANADA.

In December 2013, sixteen-year-old Jordon Cox was shocked to find out that a thousandth of the UK population were unable to eat because they didn't have enough money. The teenager from Brentford decided he wanted to do something to help families that Christmas.

He began to scour hundreds of in-store magazines and websites for money-off and cash-back coupons for dozens of different food products. Jordon spent hours at a time each day on the project, while also studying Business and Enterprise at college.

Within a few weeks he'd collected 470 coupons, which he then took on a shopping spree in his local supermarket. He filled three trolleys with a variety of items that included twenty packs of frozen Yorkshire puddings, eighty packs of butter, ten boxes of Paxo stuffing, fifteen bags of frozen Brussels sprouts and 200 packets of biscuits.

Jordon was astonished at the result when the final amount was totted up at the till. It came to £572.16, but after the coupons were factored in, the bill was reduced to just 4p, a saving of 99.81 per cent.

Jordon donated the food to the charity Doorstep, which supports disadvantaged families. A volunteer who worked at the charity said his donation made 'a huge difference to people living on the breadline'.

Inspired by the amount he saved, Jordon began helping his mother with her weekly shop, saving her more than £2000 in one year. At the age of eighteen he began working for MoneySavingExpert where he blogs full-time about money-saving deals and coupons.

One summer afternoon in 2014, a group of bell-ringers gathered to play in St Mary's Church, in the village of Ringmer, East Sussex. They were paying tribute to a local resident who would have turned ninety-three that day. His name was Ian Askew. Although his name remained largely unknown outside the county, his generous actions over the years had helped to change the lives of many young people who lived in the community.

By the time Ian decided to settle in West Sussex he'd already led a life that contrasted quite dramatically to the county's quiet leafy villages. Born in 1921, he read History at Cambridge before serving with 1st Battalion The King's Royal Rifle Corps (KRRC) during World War II. In April 1945, as the war drew to an end, he was clearing a village in northern Italy of any remaining resistance when his platoon sergeant was injured by enemy gunshot. Ian ran to give him first aid and helped rescue him, despite coming under fire from snipers. After the war, Ian was awarded a Military Cross for his courageous actions.

Ian moved to Sussex in 1955 and bought the Plashett Estate in 1965, which contained extensive woodland and agricultural land. He was a passionate conservationist and set up a charitable foundation to support the local parish and farming community. He was High Sheriff of Sussex from 1969 to 1970, Deputy Lieutenant of Sussex from 1975 to 1996, and President of the South of England Agricultural Show in 1999.

One of the properties that Ian owned as part of the estate was a large Victorian brickworks, which was still in use up until 1970. After the death of his brother Gerald, who also owned part of the estate, Ian decided to transform the brickworks into two semi-detached cottages, which became known as Jubilee Cottages, to help families waiting for a home on the council housing list.

He designed the homes with families in mind and rented

them out for the same price as a council house (then around £100 a month) for at least two years, until they reached the top of the list. Today they're managed by Ringmer Parish Council. But the cottages are still surrounded by fields and the details of Ian's gift are engraved above the door.

And Ian's original intentions for the homes have been honoured for the past four decades. The houses are now rented out for three years (rather than two) at £300, half the modern-day value of rents in the area. The scheme has been a godsend to many young couples who without it wouldn't have been able to save for deposits, start their own businesses or prepare for a family of their own.

When Ian died in April 2014, people of all ages and backgrounds attended celebrate a lively and generous-spirited man who had a genuine love for his community and the people living in it. His charitable fund continues to support charities and organisations across Sussex.

In 2017 Matthew Rees shocked crowds at the London Marathon when he stopped 300 metres short of the finish line to help a stranger complete the race.

After running for twenty-six miles, he realised he could beat his personal best if he sped up in the last few hundred metres. But as he prepared to sprint to the end, he spotted David Wyeth struggling to finish. He was on the verge of collapse in front of him.

The race had not been without its challenges for Matthew either. It was his third marathon running with the Swansea Harriers club. Throughout the race his calf muscle had caused him a lot of pain and he'd come close to dropping out of the race on several occasions. When he saw David it was clear he was similarly conflicted and on the verge of giving up.

As David fell to the ground, Matthew forgot his own race goals and helped him to his feet. He was determined they would cross the line together. He began to repeat a mantra to David: 'You will finish, I won't leave your side, we'll get to that finish line.'

The video of them crossing the finish line together, arm in arm went viral almost immediately. London Marathon showed their support, tweeting: 'Matthew Rees, of @SwanHarrierDev, you've just encompassed everything that's so special about the #LondonMarathon. We salute you.'

His act of kindness marked the beginning of a solid friendship. Since then, the two have run several races together. Both became an inspiration to the running community and were honoured with a Spirit of London award in 2018.

> **AS DAVID FELL TO THE GROUND, MATTHEW FORGOT HIS OWN RACE GOALS AND HELPED HIM TO HIS FEET. HE WAS DETERMINED THEY WOULD CROSS THE LINE TOGETHER. HE BEGAN TO REPEAT A MANTRA TO DAVID: 'YOU WILL FINISH, I WON'T LEAVE YOUR SIDE, WE'LL GET TO THAT FINISH LINE.'**

INCREDIBLE
RESCUES

The youngest-ever recipient of the George Medal was Jack Bamford from Nottingham. One of six children, he was only fifteen when he rescued his five younger siblings from a fire in their home.

One October evening in 1952, Jack's parents, John and Rachel Bamford, returned home from a night out at the fair. At around 2am their pet greyhound began to bark. John sensed something was wrong and woke up Jack. They went downstairs to investigate. As they opened the living room door they were hit by a huge blast of flame. Neither of them could get back upstairs so they headed outside and climbed on to the roof to rescue Jack's mother and the children.

Jack and his father helped Rachel and what they thought were all four children through the bedroom window. However, they soon realised that two were missing. Roy, four, and Brian, six, were still inside.

They could hear Roy screaming as the pair headed back

into the building. Jack's father was unable to get through the flames, so Jack told him to go round the back of the house and catch the children as he threw them out of the window. Jack was sweltering and unable to see anything as he got down on his hands and knees to crawl through the bedroom. As he pushed up the sash window it slammed down on his fingers. Jack persevered and managed to throw Roy and Brian out of the window to safety, one at a time.

The next thing Jack remembered was lying on the hearth in front of his neighbour's fire, desperate for a drink of water.

Jack was taken to Nottingham General Hospital with Roy and Brian. His two brothers recovered quickly but Jack spent many weeks in intensive care. He had severe burns all over his body that left him fighting for his life. His mother and sister barely left his side for an entire week.

Jack remained in hospital for five months. His injuries were so severe he had to learn to walk and talk again. Even now, the tips of his ears are still missing.

In December 1952, Jack was awarded the George Cross for 'displaying courage of the highest order, in spite of excruciating pain'. In 1954, he returned to work and joined the colliery a year later. In 1965, he married Madge Starbuck. They went on to have four sons.

AS HE PUSHED UP THE SASH WINDOW IT SLAMMED DOWN ON HIS FINGERS. JACK PERSEVERED AND MANAGED TO THROW ROY AND BRIAN OUT OF THE WINDOW TO SAFETY, ONE AT A TIME.

BRIAN KRISHNAN

In 2001, electrician Brian Krishnan was driving home from a fishing trip in Carshalton, Surrey. As he dropped his friend off home, he smelled smoke and knew immediately there was a house on fire nearby. Twenty-five years before, he'd survived a blaze that had ripped through his childhood home. But he lost his younger sister in the fire and had never forgotten the pain of losing her. The painful memories came flooding back as he rushed down the street to see where the smell was coming from. As he approached a terraced house, he saw flames roaring through the kitchen window.

He didn't know it at the time but twenty-year-old Sonya Flood was stuck inside the bathroom. Her son Benjamin, just twenty-one months at the time, had accidentally locked her in. Meanwhile, a chip pan had burst into flames on the kitchen stove. Sonya's ten-month-old baby was also inside.

Brian kicked down the front door to find a wall of thick black smoke. The heat was intolerable. He was terrified. But as he entered the house he heard the cries of Sonya and her children. He knew he couldn't leave them. Brian crawled on his stomach along the corridor and first spotted Benjamin by the glow of his socks. He grabbed the toddler and fought his way back outside, following the sounds of the neighbours shouting.

By this point Brian was temporarily blinded, but he went back inside to look for the baby. Her cries led him to her cot where she lay sobbing in the heat and darkness. He carried her back to safety, too. Brian went back into the house for a third time with a neighbour to break down the bathroom door with an axe and reach Sonya. When the fire brigade arrived, they were still chopping away, surrounded by flames and smoke. Exhaustion and relief swept through Brian as firemen came to their rescue.

Brian was honoured for his bravery at the Pride of Britain awards. At the ceremony he paid tribute to Sonya's neighbours, whose help was vital in the rescue.

In June 2019, nearly 600 homes in and around Wainfleet, Lincolnshire were evacuated after heavy rains caused the River Steeping to burst its banks. The town, close to Skegness, saw two months' worth of rainfall in two days, and hundreds of residents had to be rescued by boat.

The situation worsened as the water system at the town's pumping station became heavily saturated. As part of the site was submerged underwater, police struggled to keep it operational. Matthew Coley, a local electrical engineer, immediately set to work helping them. He, along with his colleague, Martin Reeson, helped fill and transport 3000 sandbags across the town to save people's homes and keep the station operational.

As a 6ft 3in rugby player, Matthew was used to getting noticed on the pitch. But his efforts earned him the praise of Lincolnshire's police, who took to social media that day to thank him for making a 'huge difference' to the community.

But Martin didn't only receive a thank you from the police. Six months later he received a call inviting him to the Queen's Garden Party the following May, to recognise and reward his public service.

Great British Spirit

Teddy Cushing and Kieran Delaney were on their way home after a night out in York celebrating Teddy's twenty-first birthday.

They were walking along the riverside pathway when they heard a noise that initially sounded like someone being sick. They were about to walk past but retraced their steps when they realised the sound was coming from the river. Kieran called out in the dark and a man shouted back for help.

Neither of them could see him, so Kieran called 999. Teddy searched around for a rubber ring and threw it into the water. At this point, Teddy spotted the man struggling in the middle of the river. He was unable to reach the ring, so Teddy pulled it back and leaped over the railings to get closer to him.

He threw the lifebuoy back in and, this time, the man was able to reach it. While they waited for the emergency services to arrive, Kieran and Teddy reassured him and helped keep him calm. Ten minutes later a team of fire fighters rescued him from the water, using a nine-metre ladder. Kieran and Teddy's actions were praised by York Rescue Boat, a search and rescue team based in York.

One spokesperson said: 'Without their swift thinking, there may well have been a tragic outcome.'

CHANGING LIVES THROUGH THE ARTS

OLIVE MALVERY

Olive Malvery was an undercover journalist of mixed English and Indian heritage. Her work investigating the working conditions of poor women and children in London helped pave the way for The Trade Boards Act in 1909.

Olive was born in Lahore in 1871. In 1898 she moved to Britain to study at the Royal College of Music. To support herself she wrote for journals and magazines, gave lectures and recounted Indian legends at private functions.

In 1904, she began undercover work with poor women and children in London, for *Pearson's Magazine*. She disguised herself as a flower seller, waitress, factory worker and a homeless woman so that she could learn more about how they were treated. She wrote about her experiences in a series of articles and a book called *The Soul Market*. It was a great success and is widely credited with prompting a change in the public's attitude towards the poor, as well as inspiring charitable giving.

In 1907, Olive began raising funds for a night shelter for homeless women and girls in London, supported by a committee of influential and well-known figures. In 1910, she launched a campaign to generate public interest and business for firms that promoted decent working conditions for men and women. The following year, she opened her first hostel, funded by royalties from her book, on Great Titchfield Street. Two years later she opened her second.

Olive attacked the corruption in British politics and distanced herself from the women's suffrage cause initially. However, she gradually came to the conclusion that the only way to alleviate women's suffering was granting them the freedom to vote.

In her second book, *Baby Toilers*, she called for a minimum wage that would regulate payment for all industries of work that would improve living standards and reduce the burden on charitable institutions and the state. She also addressed the issue of equal pay, suggesting that women should be paid for home work.

Her calls for change did have an impact on legislation. In 1908, Lord Ampthill cited her research as he raised the issue of establishing a wages boards in selected trades to improve the conditions of workers.

In 1909, the Trade Board Act was passed. It set up boards to establish minimum wages that ensured workers in low-paid industries received a fair deal. The Act covered chain-making, tailoring, paper-box making and machine-made lace and finishing trades. In 1912, a Board was established under the Act for the coal-mining industry. In 1918 it was updated to incorporate more industries.

Olive died in 1914 due to an accidental overdose of sedatives. She had been suffering from cancer. She was just thirty-seven.

NIGEL OSBORNE

Nigel Osborne is a composer who's achieved extraordinary success throughout his career. His works have been performed all over the world by major orchestras and opera houses and, on occasion, within some fairly unconventional settings – one of the highlights of his career was conducting the Berlin Philharmonic Orchestra in a German prison. He's also collaborated with many well-known directors and writers – Peter Sellars, Samuel Beckett and Simon Callow, to name a few.

But it's Nigel's belief that a musician must become actively involved with society that has informed some of his transformative work as a music therapist. Since the early 1990s, Nigel's pioneering methods in music therapy have helped hundreds of traumatised children whose lives have been torn apart by conflict and war.

Nigel was born in Manchester in 1948. He studied composition at Oxford in the early 1970s and spent some years in Poland as a postgraduate student. A passionate advocate for human rights, he was an active supporter of the Workers' Defence Committee in Poland and the Citizens Forum in former Czechoslovakia.

He returned to the UK where he taught music in secondary

schools and composed new works in his spare time, which won a number of European prizes. Since he was a teenager he'd enjoyed a strong affiliation with the former Yugoslavia and had travelled to the country regularly. But by the early 1990s the country had dissolved and war had broken out in the Balkans. Nigel refused to sit back and do nothing to help the people who were suffering there. During the war he developed his methods of music therapy and the creative arts to support children affected by the conflict, even while the city of Sarajevo was under siege for three and a half years.

He was determined that the war wouldn't be forgotten by the rest of the world – in 1992, he played in the front line in Sarajevo with Bosnian cellist Vedran Smailović and his opera, *Sarajevo*, was performed at the South Bank in London in 1994. After the war, he continued to help with the regeneration of the country, overseeing the orchestra Mostar Sinfonietta and facilitating music therapy workshops with the organisation War Child.

Since then, Nigel's methods have been used to support children in other war-torn areas throughout the Middle East, East Africa and South East Asia. He's also helped to found a school in the Beqaa Valley in Lebanon where more than half a million refugees from Syria are housed.

He is currently a field worker for SAWA for Development and Aid in Lebanon. In 2003, he was awarded an MBE and in December 2017 received the Ivors Academy Award for Inspiration.

His belief in the power of music to heal on an emotional and physical level was passionately conveyed in his acceptance speech. 'Every note you write goes out into the universe, shines and heals – that's not spirituality, that's physics.'

**SINCE THE EARLY 1990S, NIGEL'S PIONEERING
METHODS IN MUSIC THERAPY HAVE HELPED
HUNDREDS OF TRAUMATISED CHILDREN WHOSE
LIVES HAVE BEEN TORN APART BY CONFLICT
AND WAR.**

MARIE PANETH

Austrian-born Marie Paneth made a name for herself during
World War II, for her pioneering approaches to teaching
art to troubled youth. Her anti-authoritarian methods were
groundbreaking at the time and helped to foster a sense of
autonomy and independence in the children she taught,
many of who had been written off by society. She believed
in the therapeutic power of art and published her findings
in the book *Branch Street*, which continues to influence the
theory of youth work today.

After the war Marie adopted similar approaches when she
worked with children who had been severely traumatised by
their experiences in Nazi concentration camps.

In 1945, 300 children were flown directly from the
liberated camps to the UK on Sterling bombers. They were
aged between three and fifteen years old. Every single one
of them had lost their families in the Holocaust. Marie was
part of a team of volunteers who helped to rehabilitate the
children, at a temporary home set up at Calgarth Estate
near Lake Windermere. They were guided by the child
psychologist Oscar Friedmann, who had also survived Nazi
concentration camps.

The children had all experienced unimaginable horrors.

But Oscar believed it was possible to help 'return the children to civilisation' and rebuild their sense of individuality, providing his team could give them security and safety within their community. Ultimately, they wanted to give the children happy memories that would stay with them for ever and hope in a brighter future. The treatment of trauma was still in its infancy and some of the teachers were unsure how to respond to some of the behaviour the children exhibited. But they were all in agreement that it was paramount that the children should be free from feeling the pressures of any authority or strict orders.

The children were encouraged to explore the grounds, swim in the lake and play football. They were also given basic English lessons. The art studio was available to them every afternoon, where they were free to experiment with materials in a relaxed and friendly environment.

Through art, the children began to find a way to express themselves and process emotional trauma. After their stay at Lake Windermere, some of the children travelled to New York where their work was exhibited.

Many were fostered by English families, while the older ones lived in hostels, prepared for work and went on to start their own families. One of the children, Ben Helfgott, went on to become captain of the British weightlifting team at the 1956 and 1960 Olympics. He was knighted in 2018.

Another child, Arek Hersh, went on to train as an electrician before he married and settled in Leeds. After decades of nightmares, Arek began to write about his experiences in the war. They were published in *A Detail of History*, in 1998. In 2009, he was awarded an MBE for voluntary service to Holocaust education.

Marie moved to New York in the 1950s and lived in France from the late 1960s, eventually returning to London. She continued to exhibit her work up until her eighties. She died in 1986, at the age of ninety-one.

THROUGH ART, THE CHILDREN BEGAN TO FIND A WAY TO EXPRESS THEMSELVES AND PROCESS EMOTIONAL TRAUMA. AFTER THEIR STAY AT LAKE WINDERMERE, SOME OF THE CHILDREN TRAVELLED TO NEW YORK WHERE THEIR WORK WAS EXHIBITED.

VICK BAIN

In 1999, Vick Bain faced parenthood alone when her partner walked out on her when she was six months' pregnant with twins. She had no permanent home or any financial stability. Despite this, she rose to become CEO of a music members' organisation, and a revered campaigner for diversity and equality in the music industry.

Vick was born in 1971 in Newcastle. She moved to Oxfordshire in her childhood but returned to Newcastle to study Music and Performing Arts. She graduated in 1995 and decided to move to London. It was a bold move – she had little more than £200 in her pocket when she boarded the train south, and had no contacts in the city. But she knew she wanted a career in music. She walked into the Music & Video Exchange, a second-hand vinyl store in Notting Hill, to ask for a job. She began working as a manager after passing their notoriously difficult music quiz. Within a few years she'd forged decent relationships in the music industry and made some invaluable contacts that would help in her future career. But in 1999, she fell pregnant. The stress of her partner leaving, and being without a fixed abode, brought on an early labour and her twins were born prematurely. With the help of friends, Vick managed to raise them in the early years.

When her children were two years old Vick set up her own business bookkeeping for small creative businesses. In 2005, she began working for The Ivors Academy, formerly known as BASCA, a music members' organisation for songwriters and music creators. She faced significant challenges juggling childcare costs with her job and regularly went without the basics so that she could continue working. But within five years Vick had worked her way up to the role of chief operating officer.

However, as a female working in a male-dominated environment, she became increasingly aware of equality and diversity issues that plagued the industry. She began studying for a MBA and wrote her dissertation on the 'attitudes of employers in the music industry towards equality and diversity'. In her research she identified key things a company needs in order to grow and maintain a diverse workforce – these included support from the leadership, regular staff involvement and ongoing measurement.

In 2013 she became CEO of BASCA. She collaborated with several leading music organisations on a number of campaigns that championed the rights of British music creators in the UK. In 2015 she played a significant role in securing a judicial review on the UK government's decision not to compensate artists for private copying. But under her leadership the organisation also began to run campaigns that highlighted, and challenged, inequalities and a lack of diversity within the music industry.

In 2017 Vick was diagnosed with breast cancer. While she underwent treatment for the disease she was inducted into the Music Week Women in Music Honour Roll, in recognition of her work in the industry. She made a good recovery but decided to step down from her post the following year, to concentrate on her health. In 2018 she was featured on the *Women's Hour* Power List for her groundbreaking work within the industry.

In 2019, she released her Counting the Music Industry report. Its statistics revealed stark inequalities within music – just 14% of songwriters and composers signed to publishers are female; 20% of musicians signed to record labels are female.

The report also identified opportunities for further research and practical recommendations for government, education and music organisations to implement.

In 2020, she released The F-List – a compendium of UK female artists and musicians – in response to promoters and festival bookers who said there weren't enough women artists to perform at festivals and events. A national not-for-profit organisation, it aims to facilitate professional opportunities for female musicians. So far, her list contains 3,500 musicians and composers and over 1,000 bands.

HEROES
AT SEA

IAN BUGLER

In November 2013, a volunteer coastguard, Ian Bugler, put his life at huge risk after he tried to rescue a young woman trapped in a sea cave in Dorset. Ian, who had volunteered for St Alban's Head Coastguard Rescue Team for twenty-five years, faced one of the trickiest and most dangerous rescue missions he'd ever experienced. Although they were equipped with a helicopter and lifeboat, gale-force winds and rough seas made it impossible for the team to access the woman caught in the caves.

As weather conditions worsened, the only option was to lower Ian through a blowhole above the cave. In order to fit through the hole, he had to remove most of his safety equipment and waterproof clothing in a last-ditch attempt to rescue her. In the process he was blown back out of the hole by the sea on several occasions. He was also smashed into the sides and roof of the cave.

Unfortunately, Ian wasn't able to rescue the woman in

time and he was pulled back up. However, he was awarded the Queen's Gallantry Medal for putting his own life at risk and attempting the rescue under such difficult and dangerous circumstances.

AILEEN JONES

Aileen Jones grew up in Porthcawl, South Wales. Ever since she was a child she'd loved boats and the sea and would follow her older brother down to the Royal National Lifeboat Institution (RNLI) station, where he volunteered.

She wanted to join the crew at seventeen, but at a time when the industry was still very male-dominated – it was the early 1980s – she felt she didn't fit in as a woman. However, she did become the first female crewmember at Porthcawl Lifeboat Station when she joined at the age of thirty in 1995. She would go on to become one of the RNLI's first female helms. And nine years later, she would go on to become the first woman to receive the RNLI's bronze gallantry award, when she battled dangerous seas during a daring rescue operation.

On 24 August 2004, a fishing vessel named the *Gower Pride* called into the station asking for help. Two fishermen were stranded after the ship suffered engine failure. Aileen took the helm alongside three other crew members, on the RNLI Porthcawl's lifeboat *Giles*. The weather conditions were worsening. The RNLI crew braved gale-force winds and rough seas to reach them, but as they neared the Gower Peninsula they saw the boat was at the complete mercy of the sea.

Once they'd reached the *Gower*, the crew were able to connect a towline. However, as conditions worsened it snapped in the rough winds and seas. At this point the lifeboat was thrown into the air as it also began to succumb to the horrific conditions. After several failed attempts, the crew managed to attach a rope to the bow of the boat and begin to tow it to safety. However, the rescue was hindered as a huge wave slammed the *Gower Pride* into the lifeboat. Aileen demonstrated incredible seamanship in managing to keep the vessels apart.

Three and a half hours later, the *Gower* was finally towed to safety and the rescue crew returned to shore. The two fishermen had been saved. Aileen received the RNLI's Bronze Medal for Gallantry. She was the first woman in RNLI history to be presented with the award. In 2016 she was awarded an MBE in recognition for her twenty-one years of bravery and dedication to the RNLI.

MARY TAYLOR

Mary Taylor – or 'Lifeboat Mary', as she was more affectionately known – began fundraising for Padstow RNLI Lifeboat when she was just five years old. Her father and grandfather were coxswains of the Padstow lifeboats.

In the last twenty years of her life she raised over £70,000 alone through knitting, embroidering, cooking, making toys and collecting. Although she never volunteered on the boats, she spent many years looking after the lifeboat's crew, . In 2010, the RNLI rewarded all her hard years of volunteering and fundraising with the highest award it offers – the Honorary Life Governor award.

Mary continued to raise money up until her death in 2015.

HEROES IN THE MIDST OF TERROR

7TH JULY 2005, LONDON BOMBINGS

DAVID BOYCE

On the morning of 7 July 2005, station supervisor David Boyce was on duty at Russell Square Tube station.

At around 08:50 he'd gone down to one of the platforms to investigate a power failure. Passengers told him they'd heard a loud bang that came from the tunnel. David saw a faint light coming around the bend. Before long, he could see a torch, followed by a line of wounded people, making their way through the tunnel. He immediately jumped on to the track and ran towards a colleague who told him there had been an explosion on the train.

At this point they'd no idea that, minutes earlier, Germaine Lindsay had blown himself up in a packed carriage, on a train headed for Russell Square. It was one of the deadliest explosions of the coordinated bomb attacks, killing twenty-seven people, including Germaine, and injuring 340.

David ran further down the smoke-filled track towards the train. He could see a ladder had been placed to help people off. When he got to the carriages and saw the extent of the carnage, he knew the explosion had been caused by a bomb. David gave first aid to the injured, using his tie to stem the flow of blood. After comforting people and reassuring them that help was on its way, he went to fetch more first aid supplies and bottled water. He made several round trips of over 1000 yards, helping people out through the tunnel and back up to the station.

David returned to work the next day and refused counselling.

In 2006, David was awarded an MBE for his brave actions that day. He still works for London Underground.

JOHN BOYLE

Off-duty Tube driver John Boyle was taking a detour past Aldgate underground station on his way to work, when the eastbound Circle line train bomb exploded. He believes that fate put him there to help the victims.

John was a former station inspector and knew 'every nook and cranny' of the Aldgate line. He was one of the first to help people who were trapped in the tunnel and his knowledge proved vital to the rescue of around 500 people, which included two pregnant women. He rigged up lighting to help speed up the process and risked his own life to look for more bombs. After he guided people down the track to safety, he evacuated another train at Aldgate East. In 2006, John was awarded an MBE for his 'exceptional bravery'.

TIM WADE

Tim Wade, a duty line manager for the East London line, was also off-duty when the King's Cross bomb went off. He made his way down to the Tube and was one of the first on the scene to give first aid to people trapped on the Piccadilly line. For the next two hours he guided the wounded to safety and cleared a path to enable stretchers to get through. When he received his MBE for his part in the rescue efforts he paid tribute to the colleagues he lost in the attacks.

COURAGEOUS CAMPAIGNERS

SUKWINDER SINGH

In 2014, a writer from Redbridge discovered almost 700 letters from Sikh soldiers who fought for Britain in World War I. For the next six years, Sukwinder Singh Bassi researched and transcribed them so that their stories could be heard for the first time. In 2020, they were published in a book entitled: *Thousands of Heroes Have Arisen: Sikh Voices of the Great War 1914–1918*.

There are still very few documents about the Sikh soldiers who fought on behalf of the British during World War I. The majority came from the Indian subcontinent, which at the time was a part of the British Empire. These letters give an incredible insight into their contribution. It was a labour of love for Sukwinder and the process took him three and a half years, but he believed it was important that their experiences finally come to light. In their words he found 'struggle and pain'. As well as the horrors of war, many encountered racism in the alien lands they fought on.

Approximately 1.5 million Indian soldiers – Hindus, Sikhs, Muslims and Christians – served in WWI. India contributed a number of divisions and brigades across the world and their soldiers were among the first to experience the trenches. When war broke out, it was Indian jawans (junior soldiers) who stopped the German advance at Ypres, while the British were still recruiting their own forces.

Participants from the Indian subcontinent were awarded 13,000 medals, including twelve Victoria Crosses in WWI. Although in 1931 the British built 'The India Gate' in New Delhi, a memorial to the 70,000 British Indians who died, there was little mention of them in any commemorative events in the decades that followed.

Sukwinder donated copies of the book to the library at Atam Academy in Chadwell Heath, Essex. He hopes it will be made available on more secondary school curriculums and that it will help educate people about the contribution Indian soldiers made to the outcome of the war.

APPROXIMATELY 1.5 MILLION INDIAN SOLDIERS – HINDUS, SIKHS, MUSLIMS AND CHRISTIANS – SERVED IN WWI. INDIA CONTRIBUTED A NUMBER OF DIVISIONS AND BRIGADES ACROSS THE WORLD AND THEIR SOLDIERS WERE AMONG THE FIRST TO EXPERIENCE THE TRENCHES.

DR IRFAN MALIK

Out of the estimated 1.5 million Indian soldiers who fought in World War I, 400,000 were Muslim. Growing up in Nottingham, Dr Irfan Malik was well aware of Britain's annual Remembrance Day celebrations. But he felt little connection to events in the war.

However, after a chance conversation with a patient and three years researching his ancestry, he discovered that both of his great-grandfathers were Indian Muslim soldiers who fought in the Great War alongside the British army. They were just two of 460 men sent to fight from Dulmial in Punjab, then part of British India. Although this discovery helped him feel a stronger connection to Remembrance Day, he realised there was little information available to highlight the contributions of Muslims to the war.

Dr Malik decided to go into schools and other organisations and teach people this little-known history. He believes it helps to bring communities together. 'If soldiers of different faiths could fight side by side a hundred years ago, why can't we get on as community groups now?'

In World War II, the British Indian Army numbered 2.5 million Indian troops, making up one of the largest Allied forces contingents. In 2018, the first statue of an Indian soldier – entitled *Lions of the Great War* – was erected in Smethwick, West Midlands to pay tribute to the Indian soldiers of all faiths who fought for Britain in both world wars.

TABAN SHORESH

British aid worker Taban Shoresh fled Iraq with her family as a child, after narrowly escaping death, before settling in the UK. In her early twenties she gave up a career in finance to campaign against the persecution of displaced people, particularly Kurdish religious minorities.

Taban was born in 1983 in Erbil, the Kurdistan region of Iraq. Her father was involved with the Kurdish military who were fighting for an autonomous Kurdish state. By 1986, he, along with his family, was on Saddam Hussein's 'most wanted' list. That same year Saddam's secret police arrived at her family home to arrest her mother, grandparents and three-year-old Taban. She and her family were imprisoned for two weeks, along with many other Iraqi Kurds. Her mother and grandparents were interrogated but refused to give away any information.

Taban and her family were then taken from prison and herded onto a bus with other prisoners. Many of the adults began to scream and wail when they saw diggers alongside the buses. Taban didn't understand what was happening but would discover later that Saddam's regime routinely buried people alive during the Kurdish genocide.

As the bus began its journey, Taban remembers that everyone fell silent and began to pray. But at some point the bus stopped and different drivers got on. They released the prisoners and told them to flee. Taban's family found out later that some Kurdish people working for Saddam's government risked their lives to help persecuted Kurds.

Taban and her family went into hiding for the next twelve months until they were smuggled into Iran. However, Taban's father stayed behind in Iraq and was poisoned by a couple employed by Saddam Hussein. He was helped by Amnesty International who picked up on his case and flew him to the UK for medical treatment. Taban followed a year later with her family in 1988. None of them could speak any English but the UK gradually began to feel like home. However, it would take many years before Taban felt able to discuss her past with anyone.

At the age of nineteen she married and had a son. She went on to have a successful career in asset management. But in 2014 she began to reconnect with her past. She was asked to speak about her experiences as a child in the House of Lords by the Kurdistan Regional government, as part of Genocide Remembrance Day. She felt strongly that she needed to return to the home she'd fled and help the Yazidi Kurds who were being persecuted by the terrorist organisation, so-called Islamic State.

In August that year she found herself working with Rwanga Foundation, distributing aid to trapped Yazidis who had fled to Mount Sinjar. From that moment, she knew she'd found her calling. She stayed in the region for a further fifteen months, helping 2.6 million displaced people.

When she returned to the UK, she set up The Lotus Flower in 2016, to help girls and women, who have been impacted by conflict and displacement in the Middle East, rebuild their lives. A non-profit organisation, it provides a safe haven for them to learn new skills – from boxing to baking and sewing.

The women are encouraged to take on projects that will nurture their independence and improve their physical and mental wellbeing. The charity operates across three different regions – including Kurdistan, the UK and Germany – as well as the wider global community.

LISA ROBINSON

One evening in September 2011, civil servant Lisa Robinson was returning home from Cardiff on a train with her husband and their five-year-old son. Thirty drunken Cardiff City fans got onto the train and began to harass a woman on the platform at Lisvane station. Lisa intervened and asked them to stop. They turned on her and began to chant sexist and threatening insults.

Lisa, fearing for her and her family's safety, pulled the red handle to stop the train at Caerphilly station. However, the train driver decided to continue the journey, leaving Lisa and her family at the mercy of more abuse from the crowd of men. When they arrived at Ystrad Mynach station, Lisa pleaded with the driver to call the police. When he refused she climbed on to the tracks and stood in front of the train, which resulted in a halt to the service. This time the driver called the police. As she stood on the tracks, the fans continued to verbally abuse her and took pictures of her on their phones until the British Transport Police arrived.

The police later issued a statement condemning the fans' behaviour and launched an inquiry into the incident.

In the same year Lisa was recognised by the *Guardian*'s Top 100 Women: Activists and Campaigners.

Her actions chimed with a great number of women who were growing increasingly reluctant to ignore or tolerate everyday sexist abuse and harassment. Grassroots movements such as Hollaback! began to spring up in large cities and gain momentum as women were encouraged to share their experiences online.

SARAH CARR

In 2018 a teacher from Newcastle launched an initiative to tackle period poverty. With the help of local charity Streetwise, Sarah Carr introduced a scheme called M-card that gives young women from the ages of thirteen to twenty-five free access to sanitary products.

It was set up to ensure that girls from all backgrounds – even those that appear to be affluent – have autonomy over their periods and access to information on periods and menstrual health, a topic that's still shrouded in taboo.

Sarah is the personal, social, health and economic (PSHE) lead for the Newcastle East mixed multi Academy Trust NEAT, which covers four primaries and a secondary school. Her scheme attracted support from the charity Plan International UK who has also helped her set up health hubs in the five schools under her care. As well as free sanitary products, the hubs give out fresh leggings and tights. She said part of supporting pupils living in period poverty is realising the level of need in pupils' homes.

Sarah appointed teachers and pupils to be 'period ambassadors' that the students could go to for advice and support.

During the great lockdown, period poverty was exacerbated and the need for sanitary products became even greater. Research published by Plan International in April 2020 revealed that three in ten girls aged fourteen to twenty-one were struggling to afford or access period products. To help combat the problem, Sarah worked with Streetwise to deliver sanitary products.

HEROES IN THE MIDST OF TERROR

MANCHESTER BOMBING

On 23 May 2017, twenty-two people were killed and fifty-nine injured when a suicide bomber detonated a device at an Ariana Grande concert in Manchester Arena. In the chaos that followed, around fifty children were separated from their parents and guardians. Forty-eight-year-old Paula Robinson, a nursing assistant, helped lead the children to safety to a nearby hotel.

Paula was out with her husband celebrating their thirteenth wedding anniversary. They were at Victoria train station next to the arena when the blast struck. Paula felt the explosion and soon saw dozens of young girls and teenagers screaming and running from the building.

Paula rushed to their aid and helped guide them to a nearby hotel, where she shared her phone number on social media and asked parents to contact her. She and her husband remained with them until all the children were reunited with their parents.

About 14,000 people were at the venue on the night of the bombing. Among those killed were an aunt who shielded her niece from the blast and eight-year-old Saffie Rose Roussos, the youngest victim.

KEITH PALMER

In 2017, police officer Keith Palmer was posthumously awarded the George Medal for stopping an armed terrorist from entering the Palace of Westminster during the 2017 Westminster attack.

Keith joined the Metropolitan Police Service (MPS) in November 2001 as a police constable, after serving in the British Army. He then joined the Territorial Support Group, a grouping that specialises in public order and operates across Greater London.

In April 2016, he joined the MPS's Parliamentary and Diplomatic Protection Group. On the afternoon of 22 March 2017, Keith was in New Palace Yard guarding the Palace of Westminster. Later that afternoon a knife-wielding figure came running towards him – it was Khalid Masood who, driving a rented vehicle, had just killed four people and injured many others on Westminster Bridge. Although Keith was unarmed, he confronted Masood, giving armed police officers enough time to arrive and shoot the terrorist dead. However, Keith was fatally injured in his attempt to stop him.

Keith was laid to rest in the Chapel of St Mary Undercroft,

Palace of Westminster, a rare honour. Tens of thousands of people lined the streets for his funeral, including 5000 police officers.

In the 2017 Birthday Honours, Keith was awarded the George Medal 'for confronting an armed terrorist to protect others and Parliament'. The Metropolitan Police Service retired his shoulder number (4157U) as a mark of respect, and stated that it would 'not be reissued to any other officer'. His name has been added to the United Kingdom's Police Roll of Honour by the Police Roll of Honour Trust. He was honoured at the 2018 Met Excellence Awards for outstanding bravery.

The Westminster attack was the first in a series of major extremist attacks on British soil in 2017, during which dozens were killed.

LONDON BRIDGE TERROR ATTACK

On 3 June 2017, British Transport Police officer Wayne Marques fought off three terrorists who went on a rampage around Borough Market looking for victims to stab.

It was a Saturday night and Wayne had started his patrol near London Bridge station when he heard screams coming from the market. Shortly afterwards he saw somebody being stabbed. Wayne charged towards one of the terrorists who was attacking a man who'd fallen to the floor. When he reached the attacker he struck him with his baton, but not before he was blinded in his right eye by a blow to the head. Wayne found himself surrounded by the three terrorists who continued to attack him. Although Wayne was stabbed at least eight times, he survived the attack and returned to work. In 2017, he was awarded the George Medal for bravery.

Emergency Response Officer Charlie Guenigault was also awarded the George Medal for his actions that day. He was off duty and on his way home when he walked past the market. Charlie caught sight of Wayne and another officer at the scene attempting to help civilians. Although he was unarmed he rushed in and fought the attackers with his bare hands. He was stabbed in the head, back and stomach and had to undergo a three-hour operation to remove his spleen.

The three terrorists, Khuram Butt, Rachid Redouane and Youssef Zaghba, killed eight people and injured forty-eight others in an attack that lasted ten minutes before police arrived and shot them dead.

CHRIS NORMAN

In 2015, a British grandfather helped two off-US servicemen overpower a suspected terrorist on a Thalys high-speed train bound for Paris.

Sixty-two-year-old IT consultant Chris Norman was travelling from Amsterdam to Paris in the packed train when he heard a gunshot and the sound of breaking glass. He looked on in horror as he saw a heavily armed man running to the front of the train waving a Kalashnikov. His first instinct was to hide but then he overheard three Americans – two of who happened to be off-duty US servicemen – sitting nearby begin to plan how they were going to overpower the terrorist. Chris reasoned he was probably going to get killed anyway and he was prepared to die trying, rather than sit back and do nothing.

The armed man was Ayoub El Khazzani. He'd been known to the French authorities for eighteen months. Chris assumed the assailant had a magazine full on his weapon but it turned out he had almost 300 rounds of ammunition. He also had a pistol and a box cutter knife concealed on him. Meanwhile, members of the train crew had locked themselves inside their own carriage.

The first man who attempted to restrain Ayoub was a twenty-eight-year old Frenchman who had spotted him armed to the hilt as he exited a toilet on the train. In the ensuing struggle Ayoub shot another man with his pistol, who'd managed to wrestle the rifle from him.

Chris helped the two American servicemen and a university student friend of theirs rugby-tackle him to the ground. They used Chris's T-shirt to tie his arms behind his back and immobilise him. Although Chris was injured in the process he didn't need hospital treatment.

He received France's Legion of Honneur for his actions, the highest French order of merit for military and civil merits. He was also awarded the Queen's Commendation for Bravery in the Birthday Honours list for 'courage and calmness in the face of significant risk' and for helping to save the lives of passengers on board.

TALES OF COMPASSION

Jonny Benjamin was just twenty when he stood on the edge of Waterloo Bridge, preparing to jump. A month before he'd been diagnosed with schizo-affective disorder and didn't believe life was worth living.

As he looked down into the water below, he heard the voice of a man say: 'It'll get better mate, you will get better.' These simple words cut through the turmoil he was feeling. For a moment, he felt hope. The man asked Jonny to step back and go for a coffee with him. But by the time he eventually climbed down, the police had arrived and the stranger disappeared.

Six years on, Jonny's health had improved and he was working for a charity that supports people with mental illness. He often thought about the kind stranger who'd saved him and hoped he could thank him personally one day. Jonny had no idea what he was called but he gave him a nickname and launched the campaign #FindMike. He knew it was unlikely he'd find him. But it would give him an opportunity to highlight the issues surrounding mental health and suicide.

#FindMike trended on Twitter and his story was shared as far afield as Canada, South Africa and Australia. It was also backed by Stephen Fry, Boy George and Nick Clegg, who was deputy prime minister at the time.

Jonny was astonished when Neil Laybourn, a fitness trainer from Surrey, got in contact to tell him he was 'Mike'. Neil had never forgotten about the incident as he commuted over the bridge every day.

In early 2014, they were reunited in person and Jonny fulfilled his wish to thank the stranger who had saved his life.

#FINDMIKE TRENDED ON TWITTER AND HIS STORY WAS SHARED AS FAR AFIELD AS CANADA, SOUTH AFRICA AND AUSTRALIA. IT WAS ALSO BACKED BY STEPHEN FRY, BOY GEORGE AND NICK CLEGG, WHO WAS DEPUTY PRIME MINISTER AT THE TIME.

CHAD VARAH – FOUNDER OF SAMARITANS

In 1935, a newly ordained vicar undertook one of his first church services in the ministry – the funeral of a fourteen-year-old girl.

He'd never met her but the circumstances of her death had a profound effect on twenty-three-year-old Chad Varah. The young woman had committed suicide after starting her period. She believed the bleeding was a sign she'd contracted a sexually transmitted disease and would die a slow and painful death. Chad was devastated that her death could have been prevented, if only she'd had someone to confide in and talk to. He vowed to tackle the prejudice and ignorance that had contributed to her death and help people who felt suicide was their only option.

Chad advocated frank and open approaches to sex education that were combined with better access to emotional support. This prompted outrage from some more conservative members of society. But this didn't deter Chad as he realised his outreach was making a positive difference to young couples and families, some of whom were at risk of committing suicide.

But he felt that more could be done to save lives. In the early 1950s, three suicides a day were recorded in Greater London. It occurred to him that although there was a number for people to call in a medical emergency, there wasn't a number to call for people in an emotional crisis. In the summer of 1953, Chad launched what he called a '999 for the suicidal'. Later that year, on 2 November, he answered the helpline's first ever call.

But Chad realised the helpline needed more publicity. Fortunately, he had contacts in the press through his work writing and illustrating articles for children's comics. The flowing month, the *Daily Mirror* coined the phrase 'Telephone Good Samaritan'. The name stuck and news of the service spread across the country.

In the years that followed, several more centres were

set up and Chad handed the service over to volunteers. Their commitment to providing a confidential service that listens without judgement continues to underpin the ethos of the charity.

Today, the need is greater than ever. The Samaritans respond to a call every six seconds. Its 24-hour-service is manned by 20,000 volunteers in 201 branches across the UK and Republic of Ireland.

Throughout the 1980s, Chad campaigned on behalf of HIV and Aids sufferers and was appointed patron of the Terrence Higgins Trust in 1987. In 1999, Chad celebrated sixty years of his ordination. His aim was still the same – to befriend people in crisis.

In Queen Elizabeth's millennium Honours list, he was awarded membership of the Order of the Companions of Honour for his services to the Samaritans. He died in 2007.

One day in September 2017, Joanne Stammers was about to get into her car when a schoolboy, Shawn Young, came running towards her. He was shouting for help. Just down the road a man was trying to throw himself off the A10 overpass in Waltham Cross.

Joanne sprinted there and found two young teenagers, Devonte Cafferkey and Sammy Farah, desperately clinging on to a young man. He was dangling from the underpass with a rope around his neck. The man was sobbing.

Joanne put her arms through the railings and held on to him with all the strength she could muster, despite having a rare disability that makes her highly prone to blood clotting. He begged her to let go but she pleaded with him to reconsider and offered him a place to stay to talk things through. By the time the police arrived and took him to hospital, she had bruises all over her arm. She said: 'He was twenty-one, just a boy. I held on to him like he was my own. I would have given anything to save him.'

Joanne and the boys were awarded Royal Humane Society certificates of commendation for intervening to save the man's life. The three children picked up Special Achievement Awards at the Broxbourne Youth Awards for their bravery.

After years of suffering from post-traumatic flashbacks, Paige Hunter could bear it no longer. In 2018, at the age of eighteen, she made her way to Wearmouth Bridge near her home in Sunderland, intent on killing herself. Four years earlier she'd been raped by a stranger as she walked back home from a friend's house. She'd had enough of living and just wanted her life to be over.

She climbed over the railings on the bridge and prepared to jump, standing for what seemed like hours and feeling the loneliest she'd ever been. As she debated whether her life was worth living or not two passers-by approached her. They told, her she was 'worth a lot more' than what she was about to do. Their words gave her hope that she had a reason to live. They helped her back over the railings and stayed with her until the police arrived.

Paige never saw the couple again. But she vowed to help other people on the brink of suicide and began writing letters of hope to pin to the bridge. One read: 'Place your hand over your heart. Can you feel it? That is called purpose. You're alive for a reason so don't ever give up.' Another said: 'Don't give up on this life – not tonight, not tomorrow, not ever.'

Within weeks, Paige received messages from people, thanking her for 'saving their lives'.

Paige's work was praised by Northumbria Police and she was presented with a commendation award. In 2019 Sunderland City Council decided to make the messages an indelible feature by fixing them to permanent signs, designed in collaboration with the community.

> **PAIGE BEGAN WRITING LETTERS OF HOPE TO PIN TO THE BRIDGE. ONE READ: 'PLACE YOUR HAND OVER YOUR HEART. CAN YOU FEEL IT? THAT IS CALLED PURPOSE. YOU'RE ALIVE FOR A REASON SO DON'T EVER GIVE UP.'**

In 2010 Laurain Mosdell lost her thirty-year-old daughter to suicide, after she jumped from a bridge in Basingstoke. Determined that no other family should suffer the same loss, she began to put up posters and signs in prominent locations around the town, encouraging people to talk about their feelings and seek support. She also set up a Facebook group called Basingsigns for Mental Health with her friend Natalie Smith.

Together, they placed positive letters on bridges across the town, in an attempt to offer hope to people contemplating suicide. Within weeks the group had received messages of thanks from people who had decided not to take their own lives after reading one of the signs.

In July 2016 Daniel Picton-Jones, an agricultural contractor from Pembrokeshire, took his own life. He'd been battling depression and anxiety for years. He left behind his wife Emma and their two young children, Mali and Trystan. She was heartbroken by their loss but his suicide note left a clear request that she was determined to fulfil. It read: 'You couldn't help me, but you could help someone else.'

That year, she launched the DPJ Foundation, a service designed to support people dealing with the specific stresses and challenges of working within the agricultural community. She also set up a 24/7 helpline, which provides free professional counselling. So far, it's helped over thirty agricultural workers.

Although Emma wishes Daniel had felt able to talk to someone, she thinks he would be happy to know there is more support available for people within rural communities.

COLLECTIVE
ACTS OF
KINDNESS

In the aftermath of the August 2011 riots many parts of the UK's biggest cities – from London to Birmingham and Glasgow – lay in ruins. Some of the worst-affected areas of London were in Croydon, Peckham and Tottenham. Burnt-out buildings, buses and smashed-in windows evoked memories of the Blitz for residents old enough to remember. At least five people died across the country and fourteen people were injured in the capital. Around 100 families were made homeless by arson and looting.

From racial and class tensions to surging unemployment and funding cuts, debates began to rage over the various causes that had precipitated the riots. But as many looked on in helpless horror at the state of their neighbourhoods and communities, an artist from Worthing decided to take action in the most practical way he could. His campaign started with brooms, bin bags, a dustpan and brush, and a call to action on Twitter – #riotcleanup2011. Within twenty-four hours Dan Thompson had organised one of the biggest collective clean-up operations that London had ever seen. It was one of the first examples of how social media platforms could be used to encourage people to take responsibility for their communities and create positive change.

The violent and destructive images of the riots in the media were soon replaced with pictures of hundreds of people waving brooms in the air – an antidote to the scenes of sprawling rubble and smoking embers. Musicians and government ministers were also among the volunteers who took part in the clean-up. Across the UK other mass clean-ups were coordinated in Manchester, Bristol and other big cities through social media. 'Keep Calm and Clear Up' posters began to spring up all over the country, as the mood began to switch from fear to optimism. The riots had highlighted the fractures in British society, but it also revealed what was possible through collective action.

There were more positive consequences from the riots. A number of campaigns were launched that aimed to foster civic pride and many communities banded together to raise money for businesses whose shops had been damaged.

In 2013 Dan was nominated in the Unsung Local Hero category for the Observer Ethical Awards, for his work regenerating Worthing's local community.

In August 2015, Libby Freeman drove a van of supplies with a group of friends to the Jules Ferry camp in Calais. At the time it was home to around 4000 refugees and migrants who had fled war and other hardships in countries including Syria, Afghanistan, Iraq and Eritrea.

On arrival they found what many journalists would come to describe as 'Third-world conditions'. The site had few toilet and shower facilities and little access to water. Basic necessities such as shoes, warm clothing and tents were in short supply. Many men, women and children were sleeping on the ground in sub-zero temperatures.

Libby spoke to people who had been separated from their families and were desperate to reach the UK to be reunited with them. Their stories moved her and inspired her to take action. As soon as Libby returned to the UK, she founded the grass roots campaign Calais Action to raise awareness of the growing refugee crisis at the camp. She urged its supporters to donate whatever they could to help. Before long they'd organised drop-off and collection points all over the UK.

As soon as the national media picked up their story, the campaign was overwhelmed with donations. Within a month of visiting the camp, hundreds of volunteers were working around the clock in a London warehouse to sort through food, clothes, shoes, tents and sleeping bags. People donated other essential items that included sanitary towels and toiletries, as well as toys for the children. In total, over 8000 square feet of aid was collected and sent to Calais as well as camps in Dunkirk, Athens and the Greek Islands.

In November 2016, the Jules Ferry was demolished, but Calais Action continued to support refugees and displaced people across Europe. It's still in operation today and is part of the Refugee Council that helps refugees rebuild their lives in the UK.

In 2019, a cross-Channel ferry made a U-turn to rescue a migrant who tried to swim the Channel in a wetsuit. Staff on board the *Pride of Canterbury* spotted a man in distress in the water, at least eleven miles north of Calais. They immediately sent a fast boat to save him and changed the ship's course to haul him aboard. The man was alive but suffering severe hypothermia. After the crew rescued him, a French navy helicopter was flown out to take him to hospital.

Since the beginning of the migrant crisis, French authorities have warned people of the dangers of attempting to cross the Channel. But in 2019, at least four migrants died when they risked the perilous journey.

One evening in May 2015, father of two Antony Shields was riding his unicycle through the streets of Walthamstow in north London. A seasoned circus performer, he was better known by his stage name, 'Wonder Nose' – for his ability to balance objects on his nose whilst riding his bike.

Antony had found considerable fame from performing at the Hackney Empire and on *The Jonathan Ross Show.* But it was on the streets in the district of his home that he found real celebrity, loved by both children and adults for his entertaining act. That particular night, the community would show just how much, when they pulled together in an amazing show of collective strength to rescue the fifty-five-year-old from the wheels of a double-decker bus.

Zoheb Khalid was one of the first to rush to Antony's aid when he saw him disappear under the vehicle. Although he knew his efforts would probably prove futile, he grabbed the bottom of the bus and attempted to lift it. Two other helpers joined him. Amazingly, the bus began to tilt. Within a minute, hundreds of people were flocking to the bus from different groups around the high street – diners at a Pizza Express, staff from the launderette and people manning the desks in an estate agent. All of them tried to find a space for their hands to help. Passers-by stopped and looked on in amazement as more than fifty people manage to free the unicyclist's tangled body.

At first no one was sure if Wonder Nose had made it. But there was a collective sigh of relief when he emerged slowly from underneath the bus, still with enough strength to pull his dreadlocks from the wheels. Antony was taken to a nearby hospital where he underwent surgery to repair damage to his legs and feet. He hailed his rescue as a 'miracle' and told friends later: 'I'm lucky to be alive'.

BRAVE KIDS

A three-year-old helped save her mother's life after she collapsed, when she managed to raise the alarm by calling her grandmother.

Jodie Michael, who suffers from heart problems, fell over and hit her head one morning in February 2020. The accident happened around 7am, just before the school run, and several hours after her husband Jordan had left for work. However, her daughter Aria remained calm and picked up her mother's phone. Fortunately, Jodie had left her mobile phone unlocked and she managed to find her grandmother, Diana, in the address book. When she picked up the phone Aria told her: 'Mummy's fell over'. When her mother regained consciousness, Aria reassured her and said: 'You're going to be okay, Mummy.'

An ambulance was sent round immediately and Jodie was sent to hospital where she recovered.

Jodie suffers with a genetic heart condition. If Aria

hadn't been there to make the life-saving phone call she might not have survived. Aria suffers with the same genetic condition and underwent surgery twice when she was a baby.

Aria was awarded with the 'star of the week' at school for her bravery.

Ten-year-old Didier Levenfiche was hailed a hero when he helped Westminster Police trace two robbers who attacked his mother in their home and stole her jewellery.

Didier arrived home one evening with his mother Tania in north-west London to find two men had broken into their house. He witnessed them grab her around the neck from behind, before they tore off her earrings and made a run for it.

Didier was terrified, but made sure he got a good look at the robbers' faces during the incident. He also managed to push a panic button in their home and sound the alarm. The men fled in a stolen BMW, but the police were able to trace them. Didier helped bring the two men to justice when he identified them in a police ID parade.

Detectives managed to link the brothers to other robberies across London. In 2016 Didier was named Westminster Police's hero of the year.

AMAZING
ANIMALS

IN 2002, TREO, a one-year-old black Labrador retriever crossbreed, was donated to the British army by his owners, who hoped a stint in the Forces would straighten out his naughty and mischievous behaviour. He began a twelve-week training course at the Defence Animal Centre before he was deployed to Northern Ireland for three years.

In 2008, he, and his handler Sergeant Dave Heyhoe, began service in Afghanistan. He was one of twenty-five dogs supporting British troops out there. As well as developing a penchant for playing with tattered tennis balls and chewing old bones, Treo had a knack for sniffing out devices that were designed to maim and kill. On 1 August, while on patrol with Dave, Treo found an improvised explosive device (IED) that Taliban insurgents had concealed along the side of a road. A month later he discovered another one.

Described as a 'four-legged metal detector' by Dave, his

talent for sniffing out IEDs saved the lives of hundreds of British soldiers and civilians, and didn't go unnoticed by insurgents – on several occasions the Army intercepted radio messages that included conversations about 'the black dog'. Dave and Treo formed an incredibly close bond during their time in the Services. When Treo retired at the age of eight he lived out his final years at Dave's home in Lincolnshire with his family.

Treo was awarded the Dickin Medal in February 2010 at the Imperial War Museum. When he died in 2015 he was buried with his medal and a Union Jack. A heartbroken Dave honoured the memory of his beloved dog with a tattoo of Treo's pawprint on his calf, and a statue of brave Treo was erected in Congleton in 2017.

Initially, equine specialist Jo Boddington wasn't sure how her New Forest pony would react to visiting patients in a care home. Or, indeed, how the patients might feel about a horse trotting into their living space. But Tippy's calm and patient temperament has proved to be an instant hit with more than 200 people who live in residential homes across the Isle of Wight.

Jo, along with her husband Giles, runs Bodster, an equine-assisted learning centre, on the island. They provide a variety of equine therapy sessions at their stables for people of all ages. But Jo and Giles decided to set up the project 'Whispering Ponies' to help people who were physically unable to visit them, particularly those who suffer with dementia or are socially isolated.

Great British Spirit

Although Tippy can't communicate through words, she forges instant bonds with the residents as she stands quietly with her head bowed and waits for the patients to stroke her. Many of them describe her as 'an old friend'.

Tippy likes to take the lead and seems to have a sixth sense about where she's needed. On one occasion she led Jo and the team of volunteers to the bedside of a man who was dying. He connected with her instantly and began to open up and reminisce about his life.

The volunteers also take pictures of the residents with Tippy so that they have an instant souvenir they can relate to. Jo and Giles also hope that Tippy can bring people from different generations together. They are currently developing projects to help foster understanding and friendship between younger and older people, through a shared love of ponies.

HELPING THE VULNERABLE

SCOUTS

'Every Scout ought to prepare himself to be a good citizen of his country and of the world'.

Originally written in 1908, few people could have predicted just how turbulent the next few decades would turn out to be. But it was this ethos – supporting people and communities in crisis, wherever they may be in the world – that was at the heart of the Scouts' commitment to people displaced by war and conflict.

In August 1914, thousands of Belgians fled to Britain seeking refuge. Scouts in Folkestone were one of their first ports of call, where they were signposted to civilian organisations that could give them support. In 1938, the Scouts set up specific groups to support Jewish children who arrived through the Kindertransport scheme and welcomed them into existing Scout groups.

Their work supporting displaced communities continued

during World War II. In 1939 the Scouts helped to evacuate children, from the cities to the safety of the countryside, and organised activities to help them settle into their new homes.

In 1942, the Scouts established The Scout International Relief Service (SIRS) to assist the Red Cross, who were supporting refugees and displaced people in areas of conflict. Many Scout leaders registered their interest in volunteering overseas with SIRS and proved particularly useful with their knowledge and experience of organising large camps, teamwork and first aid.

The first group of Scout leaders landed in Normandy in September 1944 and were sent to countries of conflict as far and wide as Yugoslavia, Syria, Palestine and Hong Kong. They provided first aid and emergency relief in refugee camps, and helped in the rehabilitation and repatriation of people. Scouts even drew together what scant resources they had to set up programmes for children in POW camps in Singapore, to help give them some structure and purpose, although they risked punishment if they were caught.

The Scouts continue to help displaced people to this day. As the refugee crisis worsened in 2016, they encouraged their community to support young people and families arriving in the UK.

HELPING THE ELDERLY

In 1965, Trevor Lyttleton was working as a solicitor when he found out about an elderly woman living near his home in London. She had no electricity in her house and was also living alone. Trevor was saddened to discover she wasn't the only isolated elderly person living in his neighbourhood. He decided something had to be done. He contacted the Marylebone Welfare Department and, with their permission, visited twelve elderly people and invited them to visit Hampton Court. The trip was a success. Trevor decided to set up monthly tea parties that would bring people of all ages together. As well as the opportunity to enjoy tea and cake, they found friendship and companionship.

That Christmas, Trevor received a card from a lady that simply said: 'At last I have something to live for!' This motivated him to keep going and grow the organisation.

He began to build up a network of volunteers across the city – from drivers to hosts and group coordinators. Contact the Elderly was born. Today, the charity has changed its name to Re-engage. But it's still focused around the same simple idea – monthly tea parties that support isolated people. Over the past fifty-five years it has grown into a national network of 11,000 volunteers, who support over 8,500 lonely and isolated older people.

In 2007, Trevor was awarded an MBE for his services to the charity.

HELPING THE
HOMELESS

If you're ever walking the streets of Birmingham at night, keep an eye out for a man dressed in a Spider-Man suit. It's unlikely you'll ever see him scaling the wall of a building but you might witness him doing something infinitely more heroic. After finishing his shift at a pub, the young bartender changes into his costume down a nearby alley and takes to the streets of the city to feed the homeless. Nobody knows who he is, not even his friends or family.

Before he dressed up as his favourite super-hero, Spidey volunteered for the Albert Street Project, a homeless charity in the city. However, he found that passers-by paid little attention to him handing out food. As soon as he donned the Spider-Man outfit, people began to take notice and started asking him questions. Spidey's ultimate goal is to inspire others to help the homeless, rather than ignore someone in need on the streets.

'One man I met told me he bought a sausage roll on his lunch break. When he was walking back to his office he gave it to a homeless person. That is what I want to inspire.'

UNDER ONE SKY

Since 2013, volunteers from the charity Under One Sky have walked the streets of London at night, supplying food, toiletries and blankets to the homeless.

Conditions were always difficult for the people they met sleeping rough, but in March 2020 the charity saw their situation deteriorate. The closure of shelters and soup kitchens across the city – to curb the spread of COVID-19 – left many more homeless people on the streets. With nowhere to eat, sleep or wash they also faced increased exposure to the virus.

In April 2020, the charity's founder, Mikkel J Iversen, launched an emergency food scheme to deliver nutritious meals to hundreds of people sleeping rough in the capital. As soon as the charity began to raise awareness of the plight of homeless people during lockdown, donations flooded in. Mikkel and his team of volunteers remained committed to helping people sleeping rough until they were all safely housed in hotels through government initiatives.

TAKE ONE, LEAVE ONE

On a freezing cold day in January 2019, Stefan Simanowitz had a simple idea that would spark a nationwide initiative to help homeless people. The human rights activist and campaigner set up a clothes rail outside a church with a sign beneath it that read: 'If you are cold? Take one. Like to help? Leave one.'

He was staggered at the response. By the afternoon it was stuffed with coats, jackets, gloves, hats, scarves and blankets. As well as donating warm clothing, people could also buy pledge cards at a discounted price from local businesses and shopkeepers, to hang on the rail. On the first day, more than 100 meals and hot drinks were pledged, as well as services that included haircuts and beard trims.

The rail stayed throughout the winter. It was such a success that other local communities across the capital and country were inspired to set up similar initiatives.

HAIRCUTS4HOMELESS

In 2009, Stewart Roberts, a hairdresser from Havering, began volunteering to help people with drug and alcohol dependency problems. Stewart had struggled with alcohol addiction himself. He'd been sober since 2006 and attended a regular support group at his local Salvation Army in Romford. Through his time at the centre he saw the vicious cycle between addiction and homelessness that could often spiral out of control.

One day, he saw a video of a man giving haircuts to people living on the streets of New York. He decided to take his own pair of scissors along to the support group and began offering haircuts to anyone who was waiting for a meal.

The response was extraordinary. It proved so popular that Stewart put together a team of hairdresser friends and began to offer haircuts to people in other centres and shelters. Stewart was amazed by the positive impact it had on their self-esteem.

In November 2014 he took his venture further and founded Haircuts4Homeless in Romford. It now operates in sixty-eight sites across the UK. Over the past six years, its team of volunteers have given more than 40,000 haircuts. The charity also helps to raise awareness of the emotional difficulties homeless people face.

As Stewart writes on the charity's website: 'It may be "just a haircut", but it's the kindness shown that makes a homeless person know that people really care.'

HEROES OF
GRENFELL

DR MALCOLM TUNNICLIFF was in bed asleep when his phone rang at 2.39am on Wednesday, 14 June 2017 with an automated message. It simply said: 'major incident declared, King's is a receiving hospital'. His heart sank. As clinical director for emergency and acute care at King's College Hospital, he'd received the same message twice already that year, during the Westminster and London Bridge terror attacks. A quick investigation on the BBC's website alerted him to news of a major fire in west London.

It had started just before midnight in a block of flats called Grenfell Tower. Although it began in a kitchen on the fourth floor, it quickly spread and reached the top floor of the twenty-four-storey building within half an hour.

Dr Tunnicliff arrived at King's College Hospital in South London at 3.30am. Within fifteen minutes the first wave of what would become twelve patients started to arrive. They were a mixture of children and adults, ranging in age from four to fifty. Dr Tunnicliff was part of a team of fifteen other medics who'd been called to help in the emergency – doctors, surgeons, critical-care consultants and radiologists. They were joined by doctors and nurses from A&E, as well as paediatricians from the children's unit.

The doctors knew there was a severe risk of cyanide poisoning from foam in older furniture burning, so they were on standby with kits that contained an antidote. Many of the patients were wheezing and struggling to breathe due to narrowed airways or inflammation, caused by smoke inhalation and carbon monoxide poisoning. They were given steroids and salbutamol to help them with the symptoms and each patient was assigned four doctors and two nurses.

Although this was the emergency department's third major incident within three months, the team remained calm and organised, working throughout the night to provide care and support for the victims. They didn't leave the emergency and acute care department until the following afternoon.

The fire at Grenfell Tower caused seventy-two deaths and more than seventy others were injured. It was the worst UK residential fire since World War II. On the day following the fire, Prime Minister Theresa May launched a public inquiry into the fire to establish the facts of what happened in the tower, and to prevent a similar disaster from ever happening again. At the time of writing, the inquiry is still in progress.

Sixty-three-year-old Raymond Bernard sheltered six people in his flat on the top floor of Grenfell Tower, before he passed away with his dog Marley. As the inferno took hold there was no way down for people to escape. Their only option was to head upstairs to the top to find shelter.

Among the six people that Raymond helped were forty-five-year-old Deborah Lamprell, twenty-nine-year-old Berkti Haftom, who was nine months' pregnant, and her son Biruk. Twelve-year-old Jessica Urbano Ramirez, who was just weeks from celebrating her thirteenth birthday, also sought refuge in his flat. Their bodies were found on Raymond's bed with Raymond resting beside it on the floor.

Raymond was born in Trinidad and came to England at the age of fifteen. He went to school in Ladbroke Grove and left to train as an electrician. He would go on to work at Buckingham Palace.

He'd lived in the tower for thirty years and had three grandchildren. Described by his friends and family as a kind and compassionate man, he was affectionately known as Moses.

Seventy-two people lost their lives in the fire. The youngest was Leena Belkadi, who was just six months old. Her mother Farah Hamdan and father Omar Belkadi also died in the blaze. The oldest victim is believed to be eighty-four-year-old Sheila Smith, who lived on the sixteenth floor.

Engineer Jason Allday was off duty on the morning of 14 June, when he saw a news report on the fire unfolding at Grenfell Tower. He called his line manager and rushed down to the site from his home in west London at around 7.20am to see how he could help. He'd carried out repair work before near the building and was familiar with the area.

Once he arrived, he raised concerns that the gas supply was continuing to fuel the fire. But it wasn't until the afternoon that his concerns were acted upon, and the London Fire Brigade asked him if he'd be willing to go into the basement to shut off the gas.

Jason entered the building with three fire fighters, wearing riot shields to protect them from falling debris. At one stage Jason was in danger of being electrocuted and he was only able to carry out a quick inspection as there were fears the building could collapse.

After he left the building, Jason tried to shut off the gas supply in the surrounding roads. The gas was finally isolated in the evening and the flames died down immediately. Jason continued to stay on site until the following morning. In 2019, he was praised in a report, following an inquiry into the fire, for 'his courage and quick thinking in cutting off the gas supply that fuelled the later stages of the inferno'.

HEROES OF THE COVID LOCKDOWN

HELPLINE FOR THE ELDERLY

The Coronavirus epidemic put a stop to normal life for many months. A week before lockdown, Phil Irons from Uttoxeter, Staffordshire set up a support group on Facebook. But he also set up a twenty-four-hour helpline for the elderly and isolated in his neighbourhood who needed help but didn't necessarily have online access. With the help of the post office and pharmacies he printed the helpline number on to leaflets and delivered them to around 1000 homes to reach the elderly and vulnerable.

Within the first week of lockdown Phil was receiving half a dozen calls a day. His first request was from a ninety-two-year-old lady. Although she lived on his street, they'd never met before. Another was from a ninety-nine-year-old man who'd left a note on his door asking for help that no one in the neighbourhood would have seen.

In the weeks that followed, the helpline also helped people access other services, which included mental health and benefits. A local firm, JCB, also donated 200 freshly made sandwiches to distribute with prescriptions.

For the first time, Phil was getting to know his neighbours. After lockdown he decided to continue the service as members of the community felt a stronger sense of connection to their neighbours.

CHLOE HALL – LASAGNES FOR THE NHS

When marketing manager Chloe Hall was furloughed in March 2020 she co-founded Furloughed Foodies with her friend and former flatmate Floris ten Nijenhuis. The idea for the project started when he asked her to cook some lasagnes for the NHS – he'd begun cooking for several hospitals in London. Many of the doctors and nurses in COVID wards were working long hours and weren't able to access the canteen, due to restrictions. On Chloe's first day of furlough she made five lasagnes, enough for thirty to forty NHS workers.

Chloe and Floris set up #furloughedfoodieslondon and posted it on their social networks. They were inundated with donations for the ingredients and requests to volunteer. Within weeks, they had over 350 volunteers delivering more than 2200 meals a week to over fifteen hospitals in London.

THE SIKH FOOD BANK IN SCOTLAND

Towards the end of March 2020, Charandeep Singh from Glasgow set up The Sikh Food Bank and meal-delivery service. From Glasgow to Edinburgh, Dundee and Aberdeen, they delivered 150 food parcels each week to both Sikhs and non-Sikhs. The parcels contained staples that included milk, bread, tinned foods and pulses as well as fresh fruit and vegetables from local supermarkets and wholesalers.

Although they respected social-distancing measures, their volunteers always waved through the window where possible to offer human interaction. They also personalised the parcels with something the receiver really liked, such as chilli oil or chocolate. They also started a meal-delivery service that delivered 20,000 meals to homeless shelters and key workers.

HARRY SELLEY

Nine-year-old Harry Selley from Truro first discovered his love of DJing when he helped out a DJ at a children's birthday. From that moment he was hooked and persuaded his mum to buy some decks. He tried out his new skills at his eighth birthday party under the alter ego DJ Harry. He got his first paid gig when one of the mums at his party asked him to perform at her daughter's birthday.

DJ Harry was looking forward to playing more parties, but lockdown in March 2020 scuppered his plans. He had been diagnosed with autism the year before and was beginning to struggle with the loss of normal routine in his day. He asked his parents if he could do a regular DJ slot online. From that day onwards he performed each day at 2pm on his Facebook page and YouTube channel. Armed with his lights, microphone and smoke machine, DJ Harry began to entertain thousands online – with his eclectic taste – playing everything from Black Lace to dance classics and current chart hits.

DJ Harry attracted viewers from all around the world. He also put on an outdoor disco during Clap for Carers, which proved a huge hit with the neighbours and received 3800 views online. For the next few months he got the whole street dancing every Thursday night for the celebration of NHS workers.

CLAP FOR CARERS

At the height of the coronavirus outbreak in 2020 a yoga teacher from south London had a simple idea that would bring the quiet streets of neighbourhoods in lockdown to life every Thursday night.

Annemarie Plas initiated Clap for Carers on Instagram one Thursday when she suggested a display of appreciation for care workers across the UK with a five-minute applause. She thought the idea might gain a little momentum but didn't expect many people to show up on the first Thursday evening.

But she couldn't have been more surprised by the response. The message was shared thousands of times and on 26 March a wall of noise erupted up and down streets all over the country, as people leant out of their windows or stood outside their front doors to cheer and applaud. For five minutes the UK felt united in a crisis as it celebrated the health workers on the frontline and, in the weeks to come, other key workers who were risking their lives. Landmarks across the country – from Wembley Stadium to the Angel of the North – were also illuminated in NHS blue.

As the weeks went on, the support became even more celebratory as people found more innovative ways to show their appreciation – whether they were improvising with kitchen utensils and saucepans or assembling a string quartet. It became a welcome weekly reprieve from the drudgery and routine of lockdown and a new national ritual that unified neighbourhoods in a way they'd not experienced before, if only for five or ten minutes.

After nine weeks Annemarie spoke out to say that she felt the weekly applause each Thursday had had its day but that people could still find different ways to show their support to key workers. On 28 May, people gathered at their windows and doors for the last time to make their show of appreciation the noisiest yet.

WITHIN A MONTH, THEY HAD THIRTY VOLUNTEERS WORKING AROUND THE CLOCK TO PRODUCE 200 VISORS A DAY. AFTER LOCAL ORGANISATIONS DONATED TWO INJECTION-MOULDING MACHINES, THEIR PRODUCTION INCREASED TO 8000 A DAY.

In March 2020, two schoolboys from Wrexham planned to spend lockdown making Minecraft figures with their new 3D printer. Thirteen-year-old Joseph Taylor and his younger brother Isaac, eleven, thought it would be a fun and productive way to whittle away the extra hours spent indoors. But their dad, Graham, had other ideas. As local care homes began to run critically low on personal protective equipment, he challenged them both to design protective visors for their key workers.

The boys took on the challenge and designed their first visor, based on a photograph they saw online. Within days of posting a Facebook appeal, they were flooded with donations of acetate sheeting to use for the visor screens. Then a local senior school stepped forward to donate ten 3D printers and offer its computer department as a base to manufacture them.

Within a month, they had thirty volunteers working around the clock to produce 200 visors a day. After local organisations donated two injection-moulding machines, their production increased to 8000 a day. By May 2020, the project had grown from a family-run venture to an enterprise that supported a variety of key workers – who worked in opticians, prisons and the NHS – all over North Wales.

During the corona virus outbreak, children at a primary school in Worcester wrote letters to residents in a nearby care home. Parent Sarah Milton came up with the idea as a way for the children to connect with and support elderly people who were self-isolating. Northwick Grange Home cares for thirty residents over the age of sixty-five with dementia and physical disabilities.

One of the letters read: *'I hope you are not worrying too much and are not too lonely. If you are, then I hope this message cheers you up.'* Children also shared information about their hobbies and their favourite food and animals.

The residents enjoyed receiving the letters and after the outbreak the children continued writing to them.

At the height of the corona virus outbreak, Royal Mail put strict social-distancing guidelines in place for their staff. However, many postal workers still found ways to lift the spirits of their local community during lockdown, even if they couldn't interact with them as normal. Jon Matson, a postal worker from West Boldon in South Tyneside, entertained his customers by delivering his rounds wearing a different fancy dress outfit each day – costumes ranged from Little Bo Peep to Pocahontas and a Greek soldier. The father of two, who has worked for the Royal Mail for four years, was allowed to dress up, provided he wore his ID and company shoes.

For his first day in fancy dress he wore a red cheerleading outfit that resembled his Royal Mail uniform. Within a few days people were looking out for him and news of the entertaining postman began to spread on Facebook. Although people were stuck indoors and unable to socialise, they chatted online and discussed what they thought he'd wear next. Luckily, Jon had an extensive collection of outfits at home, normally reserved for an annual Boxing Day charity dip in the sea.

He wasn't the only one to don a variety of eye-catching outfits. In Nottingham, postal worker Glenn Walton dressed up as a wrestler, and Princess Anna of Arendelle from *Frozen*, to keep his customers entertained. In Droitwich, Brandon Clark delivered his rounds in an array of outfits from Captain Jack Sparrow, to the Genie from Aladdin and a hot dog.

In Somerset, Geoff Sacklyn still took the time to knock on the door of every one of his customers – even if just for a chat through the letterbox – to check they were safe and well.

Throughout lockdown the Royal Mail were inundated with messages from their customers, praising their key workers for lifting their spirits.

MARCUS RASHFORD

In June 2020, premier footballer Marcus Rashford persuaded the government to reverse their decision to stop food vouchers for children in the summer holidays. His passionate campaign highlighted the fact many families were continuing to struggle during the COVID-19 pandemic. The government's U-turn ensured that 1.3 million children were fed during the summer holidays.

Marcus was born in 1997 in Manchester. He was the youngest of five children who lived with their mother Melanie. Marcus began playing football for Fletcher Moss Rangers at the age of five and joined the academy system at Manchester United at the age of seven. He always loved playing football but was aware of the challenges his mother faced bringing up five children on her own. He received free school meals throughout his childhood, which helped to alleviate some of the financial pressures she experienced.

Marcus went on to achieve huge success as a premier footballer playing for Manchester United. At eighteen years old, he was the team's youngest scorer in their UEFA Europa League in 2016. However, Marcus didn't forget his past. In 2020, Marcus teamed up with the charity FareShare to provide food for children in lockdown, who would have received free meals had they still been at school.

The project was originally set up in Greater Manchester but it soon became a national initiative. On 15 June, Marcus wrote an open letter to the government requesting they extend free school meals for children during the summer holidays. The campaign gained support from Gary Lineker and politicians Keir Starmer and Ed Davey. A day later the prime minister announced the government would continue to give vouchers to families during the summer holidays. He credited Marcus for influencing the U-turn on their original decision.

GORDON REID

In May 2020, dozens of people lined the streets of Edinburgh to say goodbye to Gordon Reid, or 'Gogs as he was known', as his cortège took a route past his favourite haunts in the city.

Gordon was a sixty-eight-year-old taxi driver from Edinburgh who enjoyed playing golf, loved football and doted on his two grandchildren. Within a week of the country going into lockdown he became ill with COVID-19. At the time, lockdown measures were introduced that placed restrictions on the number of mourners who could attend his funeral. As with other ceremonies across the country, it was limited to close family members with social-distancing measures in place.

The family decided to give him a proper send-off. With the help of an Edinburgh-based funeral director they arranged for his hearse to do a tour of his favourite places in the city.

The cortege started at Carrick Knowe golf club where they placed speakers to play 'Sunshine on Leith', The Proclaimers song associated with his beloved Hibernian FC. It carried on past his local pub and on through the town to the crematorium where his service was held. During the service family members sat a wide distance apart. The service was also streamed live.

Many of his friends and acquaintances were disappointed they were unable to honour a much-loved member of their community in the traditional way. But as the hearse slowly made its way through the city, they gathered at Gordon's favourite places to clap and pay their respects.

Taxis also lined the street outside Easter Road Stadium and formed a guard of honour as the cortège passed the football ground.

Three binmen brought a new lease of life to the empty streets of Wolverhampton with their coordinated dance routines during the UK lockdown. Jack Johnson, Henry Wright and Adrian Breakwell wanted to cheer up people on their rounds across the Penn and Bradmore areas. But after a local resident filmed one of their performances they soon became an internet hit.

The three continued to put hours of work into their routines, which included dances to The Weeknd's 'Blinding Lights', Will Smith's 'Men in Black' and James Brown's 'I Got You (I Feel Good)'. They were blown away by the positive reaction of the local community and began raising money for more PPE equipment in Wolverhampton Hospice Compton Care. By the end of May 2020, they'd raised over £2000, through sharing their videos online and encouraging people to donate.

And although lockdown was a difficult period for many people and communities, it prompted an outpouring of thanks to often unrecognised sectors. Up and down the country, people found different ways to express their thanks to the key workers who continued to collect their waste during the outbreak, despite the risks involved. While some people left baked cakes, others put together bags packed with food, rubber gloves and hand sanitiser. In Devon, councillor David Cox left a case of beers with a 'thank you' note.

CAPTAIN TOM

Born in 1920, within the space of a month Captain Sir Thomas Moore, or 'Captain Tom' as he is more popularly known, achieved more than many ever would in their whole lifetime – a knighthood, a number-one single and the admiration of millions of people around the world. However, none of this was ever the intention of the ninety-nine-year-old war veteran, as he began to walk the first few laps of his garden in the village of Marston Moretaine, Bedfordshire.

It was early April 2020. The UK was just a few weeks into lockdown. Captain Tom's goal was simple enough: he planned to walk 100 laps of his garden, fifty metres at a time, before his hundredth birthday, to raise money for NHS Charities Together. Two years before, Tom had slipped and fractured his hip. As well as expressing gratitude for the care he'd received, this was his way of thanking the thousands of healthcare workers risking their lives during the corona virus pandemic.

'You are all entering into something where you are putting yourself in danger and you're doing that for the good of the people here. You are doing a marvellous, marvellous job.'

He was no stranger to risking his life himself. During World War II he was an officer in the British Army and served and fought in the Arakan in western Burma. He says of his experiences there: 'It was an entirely different world to anything I'd ever been in before, but we survived.'

Initially, Captain Tom hoped to raise £1000. But within just a few weeks, the story of his fundraising efforts gained huge momentum in the media and more than 1.5 million people had donated. Before long he was a household name who'd demonstrated what could be achieved in the face of a global crisis. People of all ages across the globe were inspired to take action and political leaders on all sides came together to praise him. Boris Johnson described him as a 'true national treasure' and Sir Keir Starmer said Tom 'embodied the national solidarity which has grown throughout this crisis'.

He featured in a cover version of the song 'You'll Never Walk Alone' for the same charity. It topped the UK music charts, making him the oldest person to achieve a UK number one.

By the time Captain Tom reached his hundredth birthday on 30 April 2020, he'd captured the hearts of many people across the nation. Tributes poured in from around the country and he received over 150,000 cards, as well as birthday greetings from the queen and prime minister.

He was appointed honorary colonel of the Army Foundation College and became an honorary member of the England cricket team. His birthday was also marked with flypasts by the Royal Air Force and British Army. Captain Tom was completely 'overwhelmed' by the honours he received on his birthday, but he was especially touched by the messages of thanks that poured in from NHS workers all over the country. In total, Tom's campaign had raised £32,794,701.

On 17th July, Captain Tom was knighted by the Queen in a private investiture. He said: 'I'm certainly delighted and overawed by the fact this has happened to me.'

DABIRUL ISLAM CHOUDHURY AND
JOSEPH HAMMOND

Captain Tom's fundraising achievement inspired many other elderly people living in the UK during lockdown. At the end of April 2020, 100-year-old Dabirul Islam Choudhury from Bow, East London was fasting for Ramadan. But he decided to fundraise for an initiative by Channel S Television that was helping vulnerable people affected by the pandemic all over the world.

Dabirul set out to walk 100 laps of his 80-metre community garden. Initially, he aimed to raise £1000 but within eight hours he'd exceeded that target. As the campaign continued to gain momentum he increased his number of laps each day. By the end of May he'd raised £216,729.

Private Joseph Hammond, a ninety-five-year-old Ghanaian World War II veteran, walked fourteen miles in seven days to raise funds for frontline health workers and veterans in Africa. Like hundreds of thousands of Africans, Private Hammond fought for Britain in World War II. He was drafted into the Royal West African Frontier Force at the age of sixteen. As with Captain Tom, he fought in Burma.

On day three of his walk, Hammond had already raised over £2300 of his target, on his JustGiving crowdfunding page. By the end of June, he'd raised £28,000.

The Queen honoured his fundraising efforts with a Commonwealth Point of Light award, appointed to outstanding volunteers across the Commonwealth who change the lives of their community.

SOURCES

With thanks to the following sources:

NEWSPAPERS/PERIODICALS

Basingstoke Gazette; Birmingham Mail; The Boys' Brigade Gazette; Bridgend Today; Bristol Post; Business Insider; Cambridge News; Country Echo; Daily Record; East London Advertiser; Global Citizen; Guardian; Hackney Gazette; Herald Scotland; Hertfordshire Mercury; Huffington Post; Hull Daily Mail; Ilford Recorder; The Independent; Irish Times; Islington Gazette; The Lady; Liverpool Echo; London Gazette; Marie Claire; Morning Advertiser; National Geographic; National Post; The New European; New York Times; New Yorker; Nottingham Post; Plymouth Herald; Scotland Herald; Scotsman; Spitalfields Life; Sunderland Echo; Sussex Express; Telegraph; Times of Israel; Vogue; York Press; Yorkshire Post

CHARITIES/ORGANISATIONS

Action Medical Research; British Cave Rescue Council; The British Library; British Pathé; Calais Action; The Captain Tom Foundation; Chineke! Foundation; Commonwealth War Graves Foundation (CWGF); Dame Vera Lynn Children's Charity; The DPJ Foundation; English Heritage; Fawcett Society; Forces War Records; Haircuts 4 Homeless; The Healing Foundation; Heritage Scouts Association; Historic England; The History Press; Holocaust Memorial Day Trust; The Ian Askew Charitable Trust; Imperial War Museum; Institution of Civil Engineers; The Ivors Academy; Jubilee Housing Trust (Ringmer); Lottery Good Causes; The Lotus Flower Charity; MHFA England; National Portrait Gallery; National Secular Society; NCVO; One Mile at a Time; Open Democracy; PDSA; PDSA Dickin Medal; The People's Project; Pride of Britain; RAF Benevolent Fund; Ramadan Family Commitment (RFC); Refuge; RNLI; Royal Humane Society; Royal Museums Greenwich; The Royal Society of Edinburgh; Royal Voluntary Service (RVS); Samaritans; Save the Children; Southall Black Sisters; Tangmere Museum; The Tower Hill Trust; United States Holocaust Memorial Museum; Under One Sky; Violette Szabo Museum; Women's History Network; Workers World

WEBSITES

aaihs.org; alJazeera.com; BBC.co.uk; BFI.co.uk; bhmm.org. uk; thebreeze.com; britannica.com; britishairways.com; caringonthehomefront.org.uk; thecaterer.com; cbjstar.co.uk; childmigrantstories.com; countingmusic.co.uk; culture24. org.uk; dambusters.org.uk; devonlive.com; doorsteplondon.

com; dreamflight.org; eastendwomensmuseum.org; gayinthe80s.com; gov.uk; granta.com; historic-uk.com; history.com; historytoday.com; historyhit.com; infed.org; ITV.com; jonnybenjamin.co.uk; jordoncox.com; justice. org.uk; kentonline.co.uk; lgsm.org; lincolnshirelive.co.uk ; mentalhealth.org; miltonkeynes.co.uk; newsshopper.co.uk; nicholaswinton.com; 1914centenary.com; olivemalvery. com; politics.co.uk; reengage.org.uk; service2schools.org.uk; simonweston.com; skegnessstandard.co.uk; sky.com; spartacus-educational.com; suffrajitsu.com; time.com; tolkiengateway.net; turbulentlondon.com; unison.org. uk; vbain.co.uk; vconline.com; volunteersweek.org; walesonline.co.uk; warhistoryonline.com; wikipedia.org; wordonthestreets.net

BOOKS

Jones, Max, *The Last Great Quest: Captain Scott's Antarctic Sacrifice*, OUP: Oxford, 2004

Malvery, Olive, *The Soul Market*, Forgotten Books: London, 2012

Mortimer, Gavin, *The Longest Night: Voices from the London Blitz*, W&N: London, 2006

Penarth, Marie, *Branch Street: A Sociological Study*, George Allen & Unwin: London, 1945